EXETER

history & guide

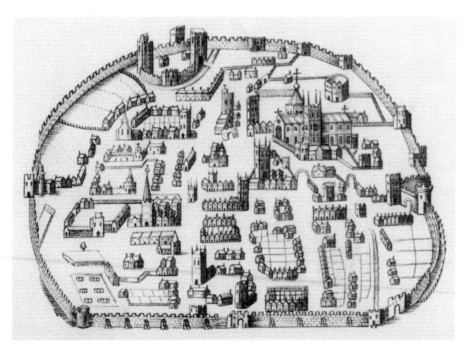

EXETER

history & guide

Tony Lethbridge

TEMPUS

Fronticepiece pictures:

Above: The Common Seal of the City, dating from between 1170 and 1180. The legend on the seal reads *SIGILLVM : CIVITATIS : EXONIE* (the seal of the city of Exeter).

Below: A sixteenth-century drawing showing medieval Exeter surrounded by its city wall.

First published 2005

Tempus Publishing Limited
The Mill, Brimscombe Port,
Stroud, Gloucestershire, GL5 2QG
www.tempus-publishing.com

British Library Cataloguing in Publication Data.
A catalogue record for this book is available from the British Library.

ISBN 0 7524 3515 9

Typesetting and origination by Tempus Publishing Limited
Printed in Great Britain

Contents

Introduction and Acknowledgements

Exeter has a long and colourful history. Indeed, the city has played an important role in the annals of England, although its significance nationally is probably not as well known as it might be. Many of the most important events in Exeter's history have occurred within a few hundred yards of the Cathedral of St Peter. Therefore probably the best place to reflect on these episodes is from a bench on the cathedral green or, even more enjoyable, from a window table in the Well House with a pint of good local ale. From here it is easy to imagine Roman soldiers heading for their magnificent bathhouse (in fact they can still be seen around the city when the Isca Contubrenum re-enactment group is on parade); Norman builders constructing the cathedral itself; the many monarchs who through the ages have visited the great church or the drone of approaching bombers. As a true Exonian the Cathedral Close is one of my favourite places. Hopefully this book reflects the great affection I feel for both the cathedral and my native city which surrounds it.

The book is not intended to be the ultimate history of Exeter and critics will certainly point to aspects which I have failed to cover. I make no apology for that. I am not an academic and generally those areas have already been well covered by far more erudite historians. I prefer to concentrate on those angles of Exeter's story that have interested me since childhood, highlight lesser-known events and characters, and hopefully separate the facts from the folklore.

Exeter has changed a great deal during my lifetime and one of the great benefits of the last thirty years has been the wealth of local history books which have appeared on the shelves to join the works of eminent historians of the calibre of W.G. Hoskin and Robert Newton. I have drawn widely on this rich output and my thanks especially go to Dick Passmore, Geoffrey Harding, Peter Thomas, Christine Trigger, Hazel Harvey, Nicholas Orme, Todd Gray, not forgetting my good friend Chips Barber. Geoff Worrall's long-running and hugely popular weekly nostalgia column in the *Express and Echo* is always a wonderful source of information. Thanks must also go to Colin Richardson, who provided a great deal of information on the American naval depot, Brian Matthews for photographs and Len Dawkins for the drawings.

I greatly appreciate the assistance I always receive from Ian Maxted, Tony Rouse and Richard Applegate, my colleagues at the Westcountry Studies Library, a real Aladdin's cave of information for anyone interested in local history.

I would also like to thank Matilda Pearce at Tempus for her support, encouragement and infinite patience as I struggled to complete the task I had set myself.

My thanks too must go to Bruce Springsteen and Billy Joel for helping me cope with long days and nights at the PC face, but most of all my love and thanks go to my wife Christine, who, after showing amazement at the size of the task I had taken on, has supported and motivated as well as correcting and suggesting improvements to the manuscript. Thank you Chris, this one is for you.

Tony Lethbridge,
July 2005

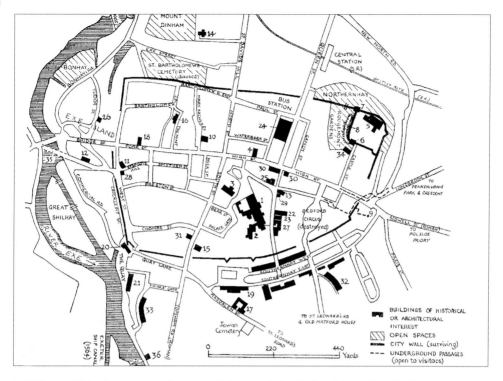

A 1952 map of Exter city centre indicating points of interest, including the line of the medieval Exe Bridge. Bedford Circus is still marked but noted as destroyed.

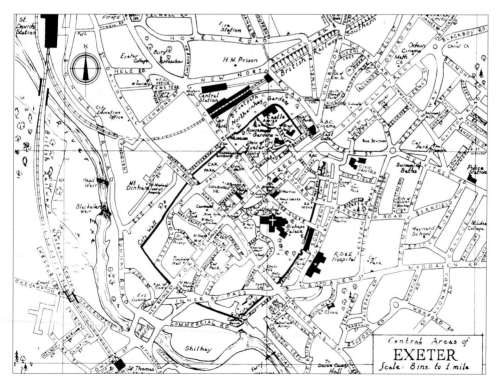

This mid-1970s map of central Exeter shows the two new Exe Bridges and the Western Way inner bypass, it also reveals how much of the city wall has survived.

one

Roman Exeter

The Romans were by no means the first inhabitants of Exeter or Isca Dumnoniorum, as they called it. South-west England from Land's End to west Somerset was the territory of the Dumnonii, Iron-Age Celts who lived by farming. They are believed to have lived around the area where the Romans established their fort but not necessarily on the site of the present-day city centre. The Celtic name Isca meant 'the river rich in salmon'.

The Romans reached what would become Exeter in AD 49. The invaders were the Second Augustan Legion, led by their legate, Vespasian, who would later become emperor. The Second Augustan was one of four legions plus a number of auxiliary units that had invaded Britain in AD 43. Vespasian had been ordered to subdue southern England by the Emperor Claudius. He and his legion fought their way west, winning thirty battles and capturing twenty hill forts as well as

A modern-day Roman soldier guards the Guildhall.

the Isle of Wight. The Second Legion's victories had included bloody triumphs over the fierce Durotrigies at Maiden Castle and Spettisbury in Dorset.

Their object in marching to banks of the Exe would appear to be to secure the river crossing. Despite making forays further west and establishing marching forts on the fringes of Dartmoor and north Devon, Exeter marked the south-western frontier of Roman Britain.

The Romans may have approached along the ancient ridgeway known as the Icknield Way (which follows the line of the present High Street) at the end of which they found themselves on a spur ending in a cliff overlooking a river. To the north the ground fell steeply down into a valley along the bottom of which flowed a stream. To the south the ground sloped more gently down to another stream. It was an ideal defensive position on which to establish a fortress.

The original Roman fort was surrounded by a ditch and the basic defences consisted of a turf-covered earth rampart topped with a wooden palisade which was entered through wooden gates set on each of the four sides. The earth ramparts enclosed 38 acres, which included barrack blocks, administration offices, the commandant's praetorium, and granaries. The majority of the buildings were constructed from timber but the centrepiece was an impressive stone bathhouse, built around AD 55, complete with mosaic floors and walled with Purbeck marble. Water was channelled in from springs situated at what is now St Sidwell's, and heated by a furnace. The bathhouse consisted of three sections: the caldarium (the hot steamy bath with cold basins), the tepidarium (the warm bath) and finally the frigidarium (the cold bath). The bathhouse was the recreational and social centre of the army post. Much of the site was excavated in the 1970s, but

Part of the remaining section of the original earth rampart.

large parts of it extended out under the present High Street so cannot be investigated. After the excavations of the seventies the site, now part of the cathedral processional way, was protected by sand and re-covered, but now at the start of the twenty-first century it is hoped that the Exeter bath house can be uncovered again and permanently displayed.

A signal station was built at the top of Stoke Hill from where the sentries could see warning beacons by which the garrison maintained contact with Dorchester.

In AD 60 the Second Legion were summoned to assist in putting down Boudicca's revolt. The camp prefect, a retired senior centurion named Poenius Postumus, was in command due to the absence of the legate. Postumus disobeyed the order, brought disgrace on the legion and consequently committed suicide.

Around this period of British resistance to the Romans legend has it that the Roman Second Legion attacked the British camp overlooking the river for eight days but failed to take it. On hearing of the assault, Arviragus, the King of Britain, marched from the east with his army to relieve his compatriots. After a long and bloody battle, night fell without either side gaining the upper hand. Darkness forced both sides to withdraw but next day Arviragus and Vespasian made peace after the British Queen had mediated. This story originated from the notoriously unreliable medieval chronicler, Geoffrey of Monmouth.

The Second Legion remained at Exeter until around AD 78-80 when they were posted to Wales, taking the wooden palisade with them. Exeter then became a Romano-British town living in peace with the Dumnonii. The military bath house was demolished and replaced with an impressive forum and basilica. The forum was the marketplace lined on three sides by colonnades of

An example of the Roman stonework in the city wall.

shops, while the fourth side was formed by the basilica, the town hall, where justice was dispensed in a room known as the curia. In AD 160 the original earth defences had fallen into disuse and were rebuilt and extended to take in a greater area. Forty years later a protective stonewall was also built, over 15ft high in places and 9ft thick, the stone having been quarried from the volcanic mound that would later become Rougemont Castle. This wall became the basis for the city wall, much of which can still be seen today along with a few remaining sections of the earth bank. Sections of the original Roman stonework in the wall are noticeable for the quality of the masonry compared with the later medieval work. The line of the wall followed the natural defensive contours along the bluff above the river then turned right along the edge of the steep escarpment above the Longbrook valley, eventually turning right again around the high ground, on which 1,000 years later Rougemont Castle would stand, then down to the East Gate. From there it followed the level ground before eventually returning to the river.

The river played an important part in the life of the Roman town. A stone ledge at the bottom of the wall overlooking the river was used as a small quay. The river was tidal to this point and beyond, making it easier to navigate. It was also much wider and edged with marsh on both sides. The river, which was fordable at this point, was also abundant with fish, particularly salmon. It is possible that the Romans built some sort of wooden bridge here.

Little is known about life in Exeter in the aftermath of the Roman withdrawal in AD 410 until the coming of the Saxons in the sixth century. Matthew of Westminster, another medieval chronicler, claimed that Exeter was besieged by Penda, King of Mercia in AD 632. With only a few British families still living within the walls these latest invaders would have had little difficulty in taking the city.

A Saxon abbey was established in AD 670 and it was here ten years later that a boy named Boniface came from Crediton to be educated under Abbot Wolfhard. In later life St Boniface preached Christianity to the Germanic tribes and founded the great monastery at Fulda. Exeter has its own saint who also lived at around this time. Sidwella was a devout Saxon girl, one of four sisters, whose father owned estates to the east of the city. Following the death of her mother, Sidwella's father took another wife who soon took on the role of wicked stepmother. The stepmother persuaded Sidwella to take food to her father's labourers who were working in the fields beyond the East Gate. Having been promised a reward the labourers murdered the girl by cutting off her head with their scythes. Legend has it that the sweetest of spring water emerged from the earth at the very place where her head fell. The workmen tried to hide the body in the grass but for several nights it radiated celestial light until it was discovered. A church was built where Sidwella was buried, while a well created by the spring existed until the end of the nineteenth century and later gave its name to Well Street. A later St Sidwell's church was destroyed by enemy action in 1942. When it was rebuilt in 1957 a strong spring was said to have welled within the new foundations.

The forests that then surrounded Exeter were home to deer, wolves and wild boar, and thus became a favourite hunting ground for the Saxon kings. The wolves and boar are gone now but deer can sometimes still be seen at Duryard, the name deriving from the Saxon meaning 'deer fold'.

The Viking threat materialised in the ninth century. Danish raiders were driven off in AD 851 but in AD 875 the Danes launched a surprise overland attack and having captured the city spent the winter within its walls where they inflicted considerable damage and treated the inhabitants with characteristic cruelty. When the spring came King Alfred marched westward to relieve Exeter. He met the main Danish force along the way and totally defeated it. Hearing of Alfred's victory and his imminent arrival, the Danes in Exeter fled the city but not before they suffered the vengeance of those they had previously persecuted. Many fled to Dartmouth and were drowned in a great storm at sea; others retreated to Chippenham from where they continued to harry the Saxons.

The Danes attacked Exeter again in AD 894 but this time the townspeople held them off long enough for Alfred and his warriors to come to the rescue. The Danes lifted their siege and escaped to their ships before he arrived, though several of the Danish vessels were captured at sea by Alfred's fleet. Alfred spent time in the city during which work was again undertaken to repair damage and improve the fortifications.

In 918 Edward the elder (Alfred's son) held a witenagemot – a general council of his chief subjects – in Exeter. Seven years later Athelstan, Alfred's grandson, succeeded to the throne but the Britons in Exeter and the west refused to acknowledge him as their rightful king. Athelstan marched west with his army and drove 'that filthy race' out of the city and across the Tamar into Cornwall. Since Roman times the Britons had lived in the south-west quarter of Exeter and for many years afterwards that area continued to be known as Britayne.

On his return to Exeter Athelstan rested before rebuilding the city's defences. The 'huge bulwarks of earth, strengthened by stakes, and surrounded by ditches' were torn down and instead the city was surrounded by a stone wall, a mile and a half in circumference, flanked by towers and with a deep and regular fosse or moat, around the outside.

Athelstan also bestowed a number of other benefits upon the city. These included the original castle at Rougemont, the re-establishment of the 'minster' or monastery, dedicated to St Mary and St Peter, as well as the privilege of a double mint. Later, Athelstan became a regular visitor to the city and on one occasion held his own witenagemote at which a body of laws were enacted for the protection of property, the administration of justice and the punishment of offenders.

Among the King's noblemen was one Edgar, whose third wife was Elfrida, daughter of Orgar, Earl of Devon. Edgar was described as a man of 'gigantic stature and strength'. On one occasion when Athelstan arrived at Exeter late at night and found the East Gate shut and barred, with the gatekeeper absent, Edgar unhinged the gates with the 'mere force of his arms'.

Athelstan was accredited with changing the name of the city to Exancaester from which Exeter is derived. The Saxons had previously referred to it derisively

The cathedral from the Bishop's Palace. The palace was built on or close to the site of the Saxon minster.

as Moncton due to the many monks who lived locally. It is believed that the *Exeter Book* was written at this time probably in the scriptorium of the minster. The book, one of only four surviving collections of Old English poetry, was bequeathed by Bishop Leofric to the cathedral library when he died in 1072. The *Exeter Book* contains ninety-six riddles; many of them are extremely bawdy, while the contents also include 'The Ruin' which is believed to be a description of the Roman bathhouse.

The threat of Viking attack eased during Athelstan's reign but the weak government of Ethelred the Unready allowed the raids to begin again. The danger quickly became apparent in Exeter when a Danish force of longships appeared off Exmouth in 1001. Word rapidly reached the city that the Danes had landed and were on their way. The people of Exeter had little time to prepare their defences, but they managed to withstand the furious attack of King Sweyn, the Danish leader, thanks to their determined resistance and the strength of the rebuilt fortifications.

Exeter was besieged for two months and within the walls the defenders' situation became grim. The city was eventually relieved by a force of Saxons from other parts of Devon, Somerset and Dorset, under the command of generals Cola and Eadsig. They attacked the Danes at their camp near Pinhoe, and although the invaders repelled the Saxon attack, Sweyn withdrew his men to Exmouth where, after burning Pinhoe, Broadclyst and other villages along the way, they re-embarked in their ships.

Although Ethelred fitted out a fleet to counter the Danish threat, his admiral, Edric, Duke of Mercia, went over to the enemy taking half the Saxon ships with him. The remaining ships took shelter in the River Exe below the city.

In 1002 Ethelred, in a bid to save the money he spent on Danegeld, an annual payment, ordered all the Danes in his kingdom to be slaughtered on St Brice's Day, 2 November. Among the victims was Gunhelda, Sweyn's sister. The following year Sweyn returned to England determined to avenge his sister and fellow countrymen. He advanced on Exeter where the citizens, fully aware of the horrors that would befall them if the Danes broke through the defences, put up a desperate fight.

Their courage could have overcome the danger had there not been a traitor in their midst. On 19 August 1003, the governor of the city, a Norman by the name of Hugh, let the Danes into the city and Sweyn's vengeance was terrible. Exeter was rapidly reduced to ashes, the citizens were slaughtered in cold blood and the defences torn down. Not even Hugh the traitorous governor escaped – he was dragged away in chains by the Danes. The destruction of the city by Sweyn and his Danes was the worst disaster to befall Exeter until the Blitz of 1942.

Sweyn's successor, Canute, attempted to atone for the cruel acts committed by his father. Canute assisted the citizens to rebuild their city's defences and a royal charter was granted to re-establish the rights and privileges of the monastery of St Mary and All Saints. Thus from the ashes arose a new city.

The Saxon monarchy was restored with the accession of Edward the Confessor, and during his reign Exeter flourished. To add to the city's prestige the united sees of Devon and Cornwall were removed with the concurrence of Pope Leo IX from Crediton, then just a country village, to Exeter with its city walls.

Leofric, who had four years before been nominated for the see of Crediton, thus became the first Bishop of Exeter in 1050, and King Edward attended his enthronement in person. This event took place in the Saxon minster and was a grand and elaborate affair. Leofric was conducted to his episcopal chair with the King supporting his right arm and the beautiful young Queen Editha his left. This trinity is recorded for posterity in a stone sculpture above the Sedalia at the high altar of the present cathedral. Editha was the daughter of Earl Godwin of Wessex and his wife Gytha who held the land in Exeter where the exiled British had previously lived. King Edward had taken a vow of chastity so the marriage was never consummated, but Editha still held the royal estate of Wonford. Earl Godwin's son, Harold, became King on the death of Edward early in 1066. He was the last Saxon king and lost both his throne and his life to the Normans at Hastings later that year.

two

Medieval Exeter

When William of Normandy invaded England in the autumn of 1066 and defeated King Harold's army at Hastings, Exeter became the centre of Saxon resistance. Gytha, Harold's mother, and her daughter Editha, the former consort of Edward the Confessor, took refuge in the city where their family owned a fortified house. The house was thought to have been in the vicinity of Bartholomew churchyard and Gytha is believed to have founded the church of St Olave at the top of Fore Street.

Exeter made ready its defences and many other loyal Saxons were invited to join the garrison. One of the reasons why the city opposed William the Conqueror's claim to the throne was his demand that an ancient tribute of £18 per annum be increased. Whatever the reasons, Exeter's rebellious population could not be overlooked and in the autumn of 1068 King William, accompanied by 500 horsemen, marched on the city demanding allegiance.

The city wall in Britayne. It was in this vicinity that Gytha is thought to have lived.

He sent a messenger ahead to order that the leading citizens should swear an oath of loyalty to him. The citizens refused and replied saying 'We shall never swear allegiance nor admit the King within our walls, but we will pay him tribute according to ancient custom'. This tribute traditionally went towards the dowries of the Queens of England.

The citizens' reply was certainly not to William's liking and he angrily continued his march westwards. When word reached Exeter of the King's approach the city council sent out a deputation to meet him at his camp four miles from the city. When they were brought before William the deputation appears to have lost its nerve and pleaded for peace. They undertook to obey his future commands and left him with a number of hostages to ensure the city's good behaviour. However, their fellow citizens still inside the city wall did not frighten quite so easily, so when the deputation returned within the city walls to report, they were furiously disowned and their action repudiated. The rest of the population were determined to resist and the defences were immediately put at a state of readiness.

William crossed the Longbrook and arrived to find the gates closed and the walls lined with armed men. He immediately displayed his authority by having the eyes of one of the hostages put out, in full view of the defenders. The only response this gruesome action drew from the defenders was an obscene gesture from a youth on the wall, which caused William to fly into a rage and order an all out assault on the city. This confrontation is believed to have taken place before the South Gate.

The Normans besieged Exeter for eighteen days. William's force attacked day after day while his engineers tried without success to undermine the defences. Within the walls the suffering was immense as winter was approaching, but William's situation also grew more perilous as with every day that Exeter held out the greater were the chances of the rebellion spreading throughout the South West. Several assaults resulted in the Normans suffering severe losses, but then a section of the wall suddenly collapsed providing the attackers with a way into the city. This setback forced the defenders to agree to an armistice. For his part William swore a solemn oath not to harm the city, and kept his word by stationing trusted guards to prevent the rest of his troops from looting. In return the citizens agreed to a Norman garrison being stationed within the walls.

As the Conqueror entered the city, Gytha, Editha and their retainers were allowed to slip out of the Water Gate and escape down river by ship. All of their property was confiscated and given to the Benedictine monks of the Abbey of St Martin which William had founded at Battle, the site of his victory over Harold. The monks created a priory on the land dedicated to St Nicholas.

William immediately stamped his authority on Exeter by ordering a castle to be built on the red volcanic hill called Rougemont within the north-west corner of the city walls. He is said to have personally paced out the line of the defences. Forty-eight houses were demolished to make way for its construction and his friend Baldwin, whom he created Earl of Devon, was given the responsibility for building the castles at both Exeter and Okehampton.

The first Norman Bishop of Exeter was Osbern Fitz-Osbern. Unusually for a Norman he was not too concerned about building a new cathedral so it

The Water Gate.

was left to his successor William Warelwast to start creating a new building in 1112. While it was under construction the Saxon minster continued to be used for worship. When the canons left the old building and entered the new one, possibly on St Peter's Day in June 1133, the west front and towers had still to be completed. The remains of Bishop Leofric and Bishop Osbern were also moved and re-interred in the new cathedral. Several other city churches were built at this time, the first being St Mary Steps at the bottom of Stepcote Hill in 1150.

The artisans in Exeter all had their own trade guild. These trades included the weavers, fullers and shearmen, the cordwainers, apothecaries and barbers. In 1563 apprenticeships became compulsory for craftsmen and the guilds controlled payments. Each guild had its own hall or meeting place as well as its own feast day. Exeter's Guildhall dates from 1000 but was rebuilt in 1468 and the familiar portico added in 1592. The Guildhall is one of the oldest municipal buildings in England. Given Exeter's position in the woollen industry, the Guild of Weavers, Fullers and Shearmen became one of the most important and powerful companies in the city and is still in existence today. Indeed, the Fullers were also known as Tuckers and Tuckers Hall still stands in Fore Street. It fell into disrepair in the nineteenth century but was restored and is now one of the city's architectural treasures. Representatives of the guild frequently take part in civic processions wearing their green gowns and caps.

Civil war swept through England in 1137 and Exeter was again besieged as Stephen and Matilda fought for the crown. Matilda was the last surviving child of Henry I, while Stephen was his nephew. Stephen was the preferred ruler by many people in England and Normandy, for whom the idea of a female ruler did appeal. However, many of the nobles remained loyal to Matilda, and among them was Baldwin de Rivers, the Earl of Devon, who marched into the new Norman castle at Rougemont with his private army and fortified both it and the city of Exeter for

The interior of the Guildhall.

the Queen. De Rivers then called on the citizens to acknowledge his authority but instead they remained loyal to King Stephen. Messages were sent to Stephen calling for his support, and he duly marched on Exeter.

In the meantime, Baldwin de Rivers took his revenge by attacking and burning part of the city, before withdrawing into the strongly garrisoned castle, which was well-provisioned and had an adequate water supply.

Stephen's combined army of English and Flemish troops reached Exeter and laid siege to the castle. They were constantly harried by forays from within the castle walls under cover of darkness, as well as being showered with arrows fired by the defenders on the battlements. As a countermeasure, wooden towers were constructed to give Stephen's men protection when they launched attacks on the castle with battering rams, while siege engines, situated in earthworks on the far side of the Longbrook valley, hurled large stones over the defences. These earthworks, which still exist, became known, mistakenly, as Danes' Castle.

The defenders held out for three months despite Stephen's engineers continually attempting to tunnel their way under the walls. Eventually a shortage of water forced them to surrender. Unfortunately for the garrison, the supply provided by the wells was insufficient for the large number of humans and animals sheltering within the walls. The defenders were forced to rely on a plentiful stock of wine, which, apart from being used for drinking and cooking, was also used to extinguish fires started by the King's troops. When the wine finally gave out de Rivers offered to surrender providing Stephen spared the lives of the defenders. Stephen at first refused but later changed his mind and accepted de Rivers' surrender. Stephen took no revenge on the city and even paid the canons of the cathedral for damage to the building caused by the siege, but banished Earl Baldwin to Normandy.

Crossing the River Exe was a necessary but often dangerous occurrence for Exonians. A narrow wooden clapper bridge is reported to have been available

The castle ditch and moat.

The Norman gatehouse.

for those travelling on foot, but carts and those on horseback had to ford the river. When the river was running high and swift, unwary travellers were often swept away. By 1196 a multi-arched stone bridge was in place thanks to mill owner and merchant Nicholas Gervase. Gervase and his son, Walter, decided to build a bridge but realised the cost was more than they as a family could meet. According to the Tudor historian Richard Hooker, Walter travelled around the country collecting the required funding, especially from cardinals and bishops, while his father got on with constructing their bridge. The task

Right: Nicholas Gervase's original Exe Bridge.

Below: Gervase's bridge.

was long and slow, and later delayed for five years until a female hermit, whose cell blocked the path of the bridge, could be removed. Walter raised 10,000 marks, which not only paid for the cost of building the bridge but also for its future maintenance.

Nicholas Gervase died before his bridge was completed, and was buried in the Chapel of St Edmund, which stood alongside it. During the Middle Ages houses were built along the sides of the bridge which remained in use until it was replaced in 1778.

On the advice of the Bishop of Canterbury, Bishop Brewer restructured his 'chapter', as the cathedral body was known. The cathedral was a secular foundation rather than a monastic body, and was still under the leadership

Prospect of Exeter showing
the medieval bridge in 1723.

of an archdeacon supported by three others. The new chapter would now be headed by a dean, and the first to hold this office was Serlo, the Archdeacon of Exeter, who was elected on 22 November 1225. The chapter would consist of the precentor, who was responsible for music and liturgy, the treasurer, whose medieval responsibilities were furniture and equipment, and a chancellor, another newly-created post, the title of which meant secretary.

A new chapter house was built from which the cathedral would be governed. The bishop donated part of his garden next to the south tower for this purpose. Cathedral business was overseen from the ground-floor hall while an upper storey housed the scriptorium and library.

During the reign of Richard I, the Lionheart, charters were granted to Exeter which gave the merchants exemption from various taxes. In return the city helped to pay the King's ransom when he was taken prisoner in Austria while returning home from the crusade.

King John is never regarded as England's most popular monarch but he was responsible for Exeter having its own mayor in 1205 (it was only in 2002 during the Golden Jubilee of Queen Elizabeth II that Exeter was granted a Lord Mayor). John issued a charter, which empowered the citizens to elect a mayor annually; up until then the city was governed by two portreeves nominated by the Earl of Devon. Only London and Winchester had mayors at this time.

Alured de Porta is unique in that he is Exeter's only mayor to be sentenced to death by his King. In 1283 a bitter feud had developed between the Bishop of Exeter, Peter Quinil, and the dean of the cathedral, John Pycot. The bishop did not approve of Pycot who had gained his position by questionable methods. However Pycot was a local man and had the backing of the mayor, Alured de Porta, a powerful administrator, who had held office for six terms commencing in 1276. The precentor of the cathedral, Walter Lechlade, was very much the bishop's man and as such was regarded as a threat by both the dean and the mayor. As the feud grew a plot was hatched to murder Lechlade, and the foul act was carried out in the early hours of 10 November 1283.

The office of mattins was the first service of the cathedral day and was said just after midnight. As the precentor left his house, the Chantry (which is now the Cathedral School), he was watched by one of the mayor's servants, Thomas the Leader, who hurried to the South Gate, which had been left open by prior arrangement (the city gates being normally kept closed at night). At the gate Thomas sounded a horn and from out of the darkness crept a party of men who entered the city.

Just over an hour later, Lechlade left the cathedral, still dressed in his white vestments, and accompanied by two servants began to walk the short distance back to his house. Just as he reached it the gang of attackers struck him down. Taken by surprise the servants fled but their cries of terror and Lechlade's own death calls brought his neighbours to the scene. They discovered the body of the precentor lying in the muddy roadway with two terrible head wounds and a broken arm. The city authorities hastily appeared on the scene and the coroner demanded that the corpse must not be moved until it had been officially viewed. The cathedral clergy, mindful of their jurisdiction over the precincts, disagreed and an unseemly dispute ensued. Eventually the precentor's body was removed to the nearby charnel-house, to await burial before the high altar inside the cathedral.

The murder of the precentor had far-reaching consequences. In time charges were brought against the mayor, the dean and twenty other people. Among the accused were both clergy and laity including the vicars of Heavitree, St Leonard's and Ottery St Mary. After many delays the bishop eventually took the case to the King and as a result Edward I, accompanied by Queen Eleanor of Castile, and three of his daughters, Eleanor, Joan and Margaret, arrived in the city to hear the case on Saturday 22 December 1285, the only reigning monarch ever to spend Christmas in Exeter.

The Royal family stayed at the castle and it is likely that they attended Christmas Mass in the cathedral, but the main reason for the visit was the trial, which opened in the great hall of the castle on Christmas Eve. Five laymen including Alured de Porta, Thomas the Leader, and the keeper of the South Gate were all found guilty on 28 December. They were all sentenced to death and immediately taken out and hanged. The clergy escaped far more lightly. Dean Pycot and his henchmen were committed to the bishop's prison but were soon released after purging themselves before Bishop Quinil and a jury of twelve clerks. Pycot however was relieved of his office and retired to a monastery. The actual murderers appear to have escaped justice entirely.

As a result of Lechlade's murder the King gave permission for the cathedral churchyard to be entirely surrounded by a high wall with five gates, which could be locked at night. These gates would be closed upon the ringing of the curfew bell. The tradition of 'ringing the curfew' still continues.

Under the Romans the River Exe and its swampy banks acted as an extra defence below the walls. By the time the Normans came the ground was drained and reclaimed. Drainage leats were dug and these in time provided water power for the growing number of fulling, corn and tanning mills. The main leat, which can still be seen today at the Mill on the Exe pub, left the river at Head Weir, the first to be built on the river, and rejoined it at the Quay. Sand washed up by the tide was commonly

used for building. The land created by these leats became known as Exe Island. The first corn mill on Exe Island is believed to have been that of Nicholas Gervase, the bridge builder, at Cricklepit. The whole area became Exeter's industrial quarter and was owned by the Earls of Devon, Exeter's jurisdiction ending at the city wall. By the twelfth century Exeter had become one of England's leading cloth towns, and the main means of moving goods was by the river.

The Courtenays saw the opportunity to increase their own revenue, and tradition has it that Countess Isabella de Fortibus built a weir that not only powered her own new mill but also prevented shipping reaching Exeter, forcing goods to be unloaded within her manor at Topsham Quay. Isabella's weir was effectively a barrier of wooden stakes with a 30ft gap in the middle. This was in 1284 and the barrier gave its name to the village of Countess Wear.

In 1311 Isabella's successor, Hugh de Courtenay, blocked the gap completely, thus totally preventing ships from reaching Exeter and also seriously damaging the salmon fishing. Legend has it that a dispute in an Exeter fish market was the cause of the problem. On a fast day the earl's servant went to buy fish. He found only three pots available but the bishop's servant arrived at the same time and a dispute arose as to who would purchase the fish. As tempers increased so did the number of spectators drawn to the dispute. A riot almost broke out before the mayor was called. He wisely declared that the earl and bishop should have a pot each and a pot should go to the citizens. The earl, on hearing of this, flew into a fury and summoned the mayor. A heated exchange took place but the earl had to back down as the mayor had taken the precaution of bringing a party of citizens with him as witnesses. The upshot of this 'pretty kettle of fish' was that the earl blocked the remaining gap in the weir by chaining large tree trunks together and also built weirs at the Salmon Pool and Lampreys, now known as Trew's Weir.

Broadgate was the main gate into the cathedral churchyard, built on the orders of Edward I in 1285. It was demolished in 1819.

The Norman cathedral had only been in existence for around a hundred years when it was decided to rebuild it. On 14 April 1258 Walter Bronescombe was enthroned as Bishop of Exeter. In September of that year Bronescombe was believed to have been one of 'many bishops' who, along with King Henry III, attended the consecration of the new Salisbury Cathedral. Inspired by what he saw Bronescombe returned to Exeter determined to implement these new innovations in his own cathedral. The rebuilding and enlargement of Exeter Cathedral began a few years later and continued until just before the Black Death reached Exeter in 1348-49.

The curved Norman apse at the east end was removed and a new Lady Chapel built behind the high altar. This was completed by the time Bronescombe died on 12 July 1280. He was buried in the new chapel where his tomb is surmounted by a fine effigy.

The work progressed from the east end to the west of the building and day-to-day worship had to continue with wooden screens dividing the clergy from the builders. While the quire was being rebuilt services were held in the nave and vice versa. Much of the original Norman stonework was demolished and used to create the foundations needed to support the huge new building.

Naturally building a new cathedral cost a great deal of money and this came from three sources, the dean and chapter, the bishop, and donations from locals. Collecting boxes were provided for visitors to make donations. Materials generally had to be brought in. A great deal of the stone came from quarries at Beer, Branscombe and Salcombe Regis in east Devon. This was brought most of the way by ship but thanks to the notorious Countess Weir had to be unloaded at Topsham and complete its journey by cart. Stone for the interior came from further afield, Caen in Normandy and Purbeck in Dorset. Records show that in 1317 stone from east Devon was stockpiled at Blackdown in Woodbury along with supplies of timber.

The City Seal, which is believed to depict the Norman cathedral.

A great deal of timber was required, as huge oak beams were needed to support the roof, while the high scaffolding from which the builders worked was also constructed from lengths of wood. Iron for making all the fittings and, most importantly, thousands of nails, were purchased at an annual fair held at Crewkerne in Somerset and carried to Exeter on pack horses.

Bishop Walter Stapleton (1308-26), who was also treasurer to the King, was not only very powerful but also extremely rich. Stapleton did not spend much time in Exeter but still gave generously to the building costs. When Stapleton was murdered by a rioting mob in London he was succeeded by John Grandisson, who, although unable to match his predecessor's beneficence in terms of money, was able to provide supplies of timber from his estates at Chudleigh, from which his episcopal throne was made.

Grandisson dedicated the high altar in December 1328 then sought support from the Pope to complete his half-finished church. His task was completed shortly before his death in 1369 and he was buried in his own chantry built into the wall of the west front of his great cathedral. Grandisson's office, a form of liturgy that he devised for Christmas Eve, is still sung annually at the start of what is one of the cathedral's best attended services.

Between 1349-51 Exeter was decimated by the Black Death. It is believed that half the population of the city died, including many of the clergy who visited the sick and took their funerals. So many priests died that Bishop Grandisson applied to the Pope for permission to ordain a hundred replacements but he was unable to find enough applicants. The situation was made worse by a further outbreak of the plague thirteen years later and when, in 1384, more people were drowned as part of Exe Bridge was washed away by floodwater.

These underground passages brought water from a spring in St Sidwell's to supply the cathedral and may date from 1200. The passages are open to the public.

Sea travel in the Middle Ages was an uncomfortable and often dangerous business but royal ties with France and Spain meant a great deal of coming and going. This was increased by the outbreak of the Hundred Years War. The small ships of the time made it advisable to voyage from the closest port to the destination. Thus travellers from London and Winchester travelled overland and embarked from Dartmouth or Plymouth rather than sail down the Channel when heading for Spain and Portugal. Therefore many of these travellers passed through Exeter. Edward, the Black Prince, the eldest son of Edward III, frequently travelled by this route.

The Prince first visited Exeter in 1345 whilst touring his properties in the Duchy of Cornwall. In 1357 Edward is reputed to have passed through the city on his way back to London from Bordeaux bringing with him King John of France, whom the Prince had captured at the Battle of Poitiers the previous year. Opinions vary on this as some chroniclers contend that the Prince's party landed at Sandwich in Kent.

In 1362 Edward III also created his son Prince of Aquitaine. As a result the Prince came through Exeter no less than five times as he travelled to and from Plymouth making final preparations for his return to France in June 1363.

The Black Prince's final visit was in 1369. War had again broken out with France and all was not going well for the English. Edward and his family were struck by an illness and returned to England following the death of his eldest son. The Prince landed at Plymouth in December 1370, but it was not until Easter 1371 that he set out for Exeter and London. Upon his arrival Edward was confined to bed with his illness at the home of the mayor. However Princess Joan, the Fair Maid of Kent, and their son, the future Richard II, went to the cathedral where they made an offering of five marks. Later that year the Prince's brother, John of Gaunt, also passed through the city.

The next monarch to visit Exeter was Henry VI in 1452. The King's visit was part of a royal progress aimed at reviving his flagging support in the shires. He approached the city on 17 July and was met at Clyst Honiton by the mayor, Hugh Germyn, and the leading citizens consisting of more than 300 knights, gentlemen and yeomen, all attired in the city livery.

The King travelled on to Livery Dole where the communities of the Franciscan and Dominican houses greeted him at St Clara's chapel and joined the procession. The Benedictine Prior of St Nicholas, and the Augustinian Prior of St John's Hospital, with the parochial clergy and chaplains, awaited the King outside the South Gate. The mayor presented the keys of the city before leading the King through the gate and up South Street, hung with silks and tapestries. The conduit ran with wine in the King's honour.

At Broadgate Bishop Edmund Lacey, accompanied by the cathedral canons and choristers, awaited the royal visitor. Here the King dismounted and walked in solemn procession through the West Door into the cathedral and up to the high altar. Here he spent sometime in prayer before making his offering after which he moved to the Bishop's Palace where he stayed for two nights. Henry held Lacey in high esteem as the elderly prelate had been with the King's father, Henry V, at the Battle of Agincourt, so his decision to stay in the episcopal palace was a mark of that respect.

The site of the South Gate with Holy Trinity church, now the White Ensign club, on the right.

Unfortunately, after his spectacular entry Henry lost a certain amount of credibility with the clergy by allowing his judges to hold a court in the hall at the Bishop's Palace at which two men were sentenced to death for treason. The decision to stage the trial in the palace upset the bishop and his clergy who protested that it compromised the church's rights of sanctuary. To pacify his critics the King pardoned the condemned men, but the unfortunate incident did nothing to improve his standing.

Within a year Henry was suffering from a mental illness and was deposed by the Yorkist Edward IV. Edward arrived in Exeter on 14 April 1470 in hot pursuit of Richard Neville, the Earl of Warwick, known as the Kingmaker. Warwick had previously supported Edward's bid for power but had quarrelled over the King's policy towards France. Warwick, accompanied by the Duke of Clarence, had eluded Edward in the north and fled through Exeter to Dartmouth where they escaped by ship.

Edward and his army raced after them, marching the 290 miles from York in just eighteen days. The King was much displeased to discover that his quarry had escaped, and was also unhappy that Exeter had supported the cause of Henry VI and withstood a twelve day siege by Edward's supporter Sir William Courtenay of Powderham. Courtenay and Lord William Bonville of Shute had fought a skirmish at Clyst Heath. According to Victorian historian T.J. Northy, Bonville had come off worst and taken refuge within Exeter's walls. Courtenay had pursued but found the gates of Exeter shut against him. And in Northy's view, given the ongoing feud between the Courtenays and Exeter this had 'put the city down even a few pegs lower than before in his estimation'.

However, Edward attempted to conciliate local feelings and after being met by the mayor and 400 citizens in red gowns at Livery Dole, accepted a gift of a purse containing 100 nobles. At the East Gate the city keys and maces were also presented, but graciously returned by the King.

The following day was Palm Sunday and King Edward took part in the customary procession around the Cathedral Close and surrounding streets. It is thought he may even have carried the blessed palm. Bishop Stapleton's register

The city wall from the north.

records that the procession was extended beyond the East Gate to enable all the people to see their sovereign.

After dinner on the following Tuesday Edward left Exeter after 'giving great thanks to the Mayor for his entertainment, as also showing himself very loving and bountiful to the people'. Before leaving, the King presented his sword to the city.

The balance of power in the Wars of the Roses then took another twist. Four months later Warwick and Clarence came through Exeter again on their way to London where they succeeded in returning Henry VI to the throne. Edward fled to Holland but returned in the following spring and defeated Warwick at the Battle of Barnet to reclaim the crown.

In a last ditch attempt to save the throne for Henry, his Queen, Margaret of Anjou, and her son Edward, Prince of Wales, crossed the Channel from France. They landed at Weymouth and reached Exeter in late April 1471. From Exeter they travelled to Tewkesbury where they were defeated in battle by Edward on 4 May. The Prince of Wales was killed in the battle and shortly afterwards Henry VI was murdered in the Tower of London.

Edward IV died on 9 April 1483, and Richard of York claimed the throne following the disappearance of the thirteen-year-old Edward V and his brother in the Tower of London. It was not a popular move and resulted in a spate of uprisings in the South during the autumn. In Devon the opposition to Richard was led by Sir Edward Courtenay and his brother Peter, then Bishop of Exeter, the Archdeacon of Exeter and the Abbot of Buckland who all declared for Henry, Duke of Richmond. The uprisings were uncoordinated and Richard quickly moved to crush them:

> My gracious sovereign, now in Devonshire,
> As I by friends am well advertised,
> Sir Edward Courtenay, and the haughty prelate,
> Bishop of Exeter, his elder brother,
> With many more confederates, are in arms.
>
> (William Shakespeare, *Richard III*, Act 4 Scene 4)

Richard III at East Gate, 1483.

Warning of the King's approach gave the conspirators time to escape to France, but when Richard reached Exeter on 8 November he lodged himself in the Bishop's Palace, which he discovered was extremely well provisioned.

Richard and his retinue were welcomed at the East Gate by the mayor, John Atwill, and the chamber. The recorder, Thomas Hexte, had presented the King with a congratulatory address and a purse containing 200 nobles.

Not everyone was pleased to see the King. Richard's brother in law, Sir Thomas St Leger, and Thomas Rame had been found guilty of treason at Torrington and were brought to Exeter where they were beheaded at Carfoix.

Atwill, the mayor, also had a nasty moment whilst showing the King around the city. Richard asked Atwill the name of the castle. When he was told 'Rougemont', the King trembled and turned pale, for he had mistaken the name for Richmond:

> Richmond! When I was last at Exeter,
> The mayor in courtesy showed me the Castle,
> And called it Rougemont; at which name I started,
> Because a bard of Ireland told me once,
> I should not live long after I saw Richmond.
> (William Shakespeare, *Richard III*, Act 4 Scene 2)

Although this story may have been contrived by Shakespeare to discredit Richard for the benefit of Tudor propaganda the prediction came true at Bosworth Field on 22 August 1485. Bishop Courtenay was present to see Richard's downfall and the Duke of Richmond become King Henry VII. Courtenay would be returned to his bishopric before going on to become Bishop of Winchester and one of Henry's chief ministers.

three

The Tudors

Bosworth Field marked the end of the Wars of the Roses, but Henry Tudor now had to crush further plots and rebellions before his kingdom was finally secure. Exeter found itself involved in two of these rebellions.

In the spring of 1497 the Cornish rebelled against taxes levied to wage war against the Scots, a cause they considered had nothing to do with them. They marched to London but en route were denied entry to Exeter. The mayor had expected support from the county lords but when none was forthcoming allowed the Cornish captains to pass through the city, but made their men detour around the walls. The Cornish were later defeated by the King's army at the Battle of Blackheath in June and the leaders executed.

A second rebellion followed later in the year when the pretender Perkin Warbeck, claiming to be the Duke of York, the younger of the little princes who had mysteriously disappeared in the Tower of London, along with Edward V, landed at Whitsand Bay near Plymouth. He marched across Devon and attacked Exeter on 17 September with a force of 4-5,000 men. His soldiers attempted to burn

The North Gate under attack from Perkin Warbeck's rebels in 1497.

Left: Exonians defend the West Gate from Warbeck's rebels.

Below: The north tower of the cathedral. In 1497 the Treasurer's House adjoined the tower. It was from this house that Henry VII pardoned Perkin Warbeck's rebels.

the North Gate but after suffering heavy losses succeeded in breaking through the East Gate and fought their way down to Castle Lane. Here the defenders staged a bloody counter-attack and successfully drove Warbeck's men up the High Street and out of the city. Warbeck withdrew to Taunton where he ran into the King's army and surrendered. Henry arrived in Exeter on 7 October bringing the rebel leader with him as a prisoner.

The King lodged in the Treasurer's House which, until 1798, adjoined the north tower of the cathedral. The outline of the eaves can still be seen today. Henry had come to Exeter to thank the citizens for their loyalty and also to deal with Warbeck's rebels. The ringleaders were swiftly condemned and executed. They suffered the horrific punishment of being hanged, then, while still alive, drawn and quartered outside the city walls on Southernhay. The King however was more lenient towards the other Cornish rebels who were dealt with in the Cathedral Close. A large window was cut in the wall of the Treasurer's House and eight trees felled to make space in front of it. The King stood at the window and the prisoners, with halters already around their necks, were drawn up before him. On seeing Henry they fell to their knees and pleaded for mercy. After admonishing them the King pardoned them all after which they gave a great shout of 'God save the King' and threw off the nooses. Warbeck was sent to the Tower of London. Henry stayed in Exeter for almost a month but before leaving he acknowledged his debt by presenting the city with his sword and cap of maintenance which he commanded should be carried before the mayor on all public occasions 'from the time being forever'. The tradition has proudly continued to the present day and the sword is presented whenever the reigning sovereign visits the city. It is duly touched then handed back.

Below left: The site of the East Gate. Henry VII is depicted on the wall

Below right: The north side of the cathedral.

In October 1501, the Spanish Infanta, fifteen-year-old Princess Catherine of Aragon, landed at Plymouth en route for London where she would marry Henry VII's eldest son, Prince Arthur. Travelling via Tavistock, Okehampton

The West Front of Exeter Cathedral with St Mary Major in the foreground. It was here that Catherine of Aragon's sleep was interrupted by the church's noisy weathervane.

and Crediton, Catherine broke her journey for several days in Exeter where she stayed at the deanery. Her stay coincided with the autumn equinox and the weather was extremely stormy. During one gale the princess' sleep was disturbed by the creaking and squeaking of the weathervane on top of the spire of nearby St Mary Major church. A workman was immediately dispatched to climb, in the darkness, to the top of the spire and remove the offending weathervane. When Catherine continued her journey to London on 17 October the story goes that the workman made a second ascent of the spire, this time to replace the weathervane.

Catherine married Arthur on 14 November, but the following April he died, aged only fifteen. Subsequently she married his brother and thus became the first wife of Henry VIII.

Henry VIII never travelled to Exeter but the Reformation was certainly felt in the city thanks to the arrival of a teacher, Thomas Benet, who came to Exeter from Torrington and opened a small school at Smythen Street in 1525. Benet originated from Cambridge where he had attended the university but his friendship with Bilney, later martyred for his beliefs, forced him to move to Devon. Six years after Benet arrived in Exeter notices of a Lutheran nature claiming that 'the Pope is the Antichrist and we ought to worship God not the saints' were found attached to the cathedral doors. It was immediately apparent that a heretic was loose within the city. The bishop and clergy became 'as angry as wasps' and the unknown heretic was duly excommunicated with bell, book and candle at a service in the cathedral. Benet is believed to have been present and almost gave himself away by laughing at the proceedings. A week later a boy was caught attaching another document at the Little Stile Gate, an entrance to the Close from South Street. The boy was taken to the mayor where he admitted that he was acting on the orders of his master. Benet was soon traced as the culprit and arrested. He was condemned to death but the mayor

East Gate from the inside. It was rebuilt in 1511 following the earlier attack by Perkin Warbeck's followers. It was demolished in 1784 to ease the flow of traffic.

refused to allow the execution to take place at Southernhay and instead Benet was handed over to the Sheriff of Devon and burnt as a heretic at Livery Dole on 15 January 1532. Prior to his execution Benet was given the opportunity to recant but refused. As he was being chained to the stake two gentlemen, Thomas Carew and John Burnthouse, tried again to persuade Benet to recant. Burnthouse became so angry by his refusals that he thrust a burning furze bush into Benet's mouth demanding that he 'Pray to our Lady or by God I will make thee do it.' Surprisingly in the circumstances Benet was able to reply, 'Alas Sir, trouble me not', at which point the wooden faggots surrounding him were set ablaze. Three years later Henry VIII broke with Rome and within twenty years worship of the saints was banned by the Church of England.

Benet is commemorated by the Almshouses at Livery Dole and also by the Martyrs' Memorial in Demark Road. When the site for the present Almshouses was being excavated in 1851 the iron ring and chain which bound heretics to the stake was uncovered.

In 1535 the King dissolved the monasteries and the Bishop of Dover was sent to oversee the work. St Nicholas Priory was partly demolished and the stone used to make repairs to Exe Bridge, bits of which had been washed away by floodwater, while other stones were used to build a new wool market in South Street. The land owned by the Grey Friars went to John Hull of Larkbeare, a marmalade importer who supplied his produce to both the King and the Countess of Devon, while Lord John Russell was given the responsibility for overseeing the reformation in Devon and was granted the Dominican house near the cathedral which he renamed Bedford House.

Two years later, in 1537, Henry VIII granted a charter which created Exeter as a county in its own right and separate to Devon. The parishes of St David's and St Sidwell's although technically outside the city walls were included, but not the castle.

35

Left: The iron ring and chain with which Thomas Benet was bound to the stake in 1532.

Below: Livery Dole chapel, the site of Benet's execution.

Exeter's long-standing grievance regarding the Countess Weir was finally resolved in favour of the city when Henry Courtenay, until then a favourite of the King, was accused of treason. Courtenay had been named as Henry's heir before the King's children were born but in January 1556 he was executed. His son Edward remained in the Tower of London for fourteen years but was created Earl of Devon by Queen Mary. On Henry Courtney's death his possession reverted to the crown and Exeter was finally granted permission to demolish the weir. This proved a harder task than expected so instead it was decided to bypass it with a canal. John Trew was the engineer given this task and on the advice of Francis Drake attempts were made to enlarge the mill leat below Countess Wear village, but this was prevented by the presence of rock so a different route through the softer ground on the western bank of the Exe was followed. The original canal was 3,120 yards in length and re-entered the river at Matford Brook.

The effects of the Reformation continued to be seen during the short reign of Edward VI. The young king replaced the Latin Mass book with the English Book of Common Prayer. It was introduced on Whitsunday 1549 and immediately caused a furore with protests from within the congregations. In Cornwall the imposition of the English language was greatly resented and a band of protestors set out for London to make their feeling felt. Their numbers grew as they travelled east, and once across the Tamar were joined on their march by angry Devonians who also resented the loss of the Latin Mass. The Prayer Book rebellion, as this protest would become known, arrived at Exeter on 2 July 1549, 2000 strong hoping to gain further support and food from the citizens. But the city gates were firmly shut against them. The angry rebels tried to burn down the gates and lay siege to the city. The vicar of St Thomas, Robert Welshe, himself a Cornishman, tried to dissuade them from further violence. They used St Sidwell's church to hold prisoners, among them Sir Walter Raleigh's father, and tried to cut off the water supply to the city. The siege lasted for five weeks by which time the inhabitants were reduced to eating horsemeat. Sallies were made from within the walls to burn down houses which were giving the rebels cover, while earthworks were constructed to strengthen the walls. John Newcombe, a resident of Teignmouth was caught up in the siege, and while walking in the West Quarter heard strange noises and discovered that the rebels were undermining the West Gate which they intended to blow up with barrels of gunpowder. A countermine was sunk

An attack on Exeter's West Gate during the Prayer Book Rebellion of 1549.

which broke through into the chamber where the powder was primed waiting to be fired. Containers were collected and filled with water which was poured down the shaft simultaneously thus soaking the gunpowder and rendering it useless. The defenders efforts were aided by a heavy shower of rain which helped to flood the rebels' tunnel.

Eventually Lord John Russell arrived having fought a series of skirmishes with the rebels at Feniton Bridge, Woodbury Common, Clyst St Mary and Clyst Heath. Russell reached Exeter on 6 August and immediately set about bringing supplies from the surrounding villages to feed the hungry Exonians. Most of the surviving rebels were sent home to Cornwall but Robert Welshe was condemned to death as a traitor, despite dissuading the rebels from firing the city. Welshe was hanged from his own St Thomas church tower in full vestments. Afterwards his corpse was coated in tar and left hanging for four years as an example. The King showed his gratitude for Exeter's loyalty by returning to the city the manor of Exe Island of which it had been dispossessed at the time of the Norman Conquest.

When Edward VI died at the age of sixteen, and was succeeded by his sister 'Bloody' Mary, the tables were turned in favour of the Catholics. When the news reached Exeter that Mary was Queen in July 1553 the Bishop Miles Coverdale, who had translated the whole Bible into English for Henry VIII in 1538, was preaching in the cathedral. He hastily left the pulpit and fled the country. Not so lucky was Agnes Prest, a zealous Protestant who fell victim of religious persecution. She was driven from her home in Launceston by her Catholic husband and children who betrayed her to Dr Turberville, the new bishop. When examined in his prison she steadfastly refused to acknowledge the transubstantiation of the host at the Eucharist and was subsequently burnt alive at Southernhay.

View of Exeter with St Thomas church in foreground and ships at the Quay.

Mary died and was succeeded by Elizabeth I in 1558. Bishop Turberville was promptly removed from his see and replaced by William Alleigh, while the recently replaced images of the saints were removed from the cathedral and burnt on a bonfire. Religious persecution did not cease under Good Queen Bess and in 1599 James Dowdall became a Catholic martyr when he denied the Queen's spiritual supremacy and was hanged, drawn and quartered at the castle.

On a lighter note the city council, in November 1568, agreed that 'three Common Jakes (public lavatories) shall be made within this city'. Sanitation was virtually non-existent in Exeter. Most houses had an outside privy pit but sewage ran in the streets washed away only by heavy rain. These unsavoury conditions frequently led to outbreaks of plague. In 1586 an outbreak in the unsanitary Southgate prison was transmitted to the court resulting in the demise of the judge, several magistrates, eleven jurymen, many constables and several others who happened to be present.

Elizabeth never visited Exeter but was responsible for its motto *Semper Fidelis* when she wrote to thank the 'ever faithful' city for its loyalty in supplying three ships to meet the threat of the Spanish Armada. Many of the most famous Elizabethan sea-dogs, Francis Drake, Walter Raleigh, Humphrey Gilbert and Hawkins regularly met to exchange and hear the news in what would become Mol's Coffee House in the Cathedral Close. Drake is also said to have frequented the Shippe Inn in St Martin's Lane.

Other Exonians who became prominent in Elizabethan England were Sir Thomas Bodley (1545-1613), the son of a printer, a distinguished diplomat who founded the Bodleian Library in Oxford, and Nicholas Hilliard (1547-1619), the first great painter of miniature portraits who, at twenty-four, became Queen Elizabeth's goldsmith.

The Snayle Tower was the name given to the angle of the city wall in the north west corner. A tower was recorded here in 1348 and is recalled in the name of this nearby house.

Mol's Coffee House where Drake and his contemporaries met to discuss news in Tudor times.

The seventeenth century saw Exeter's woollen trade steadily expanding with exports going not just to Europe but also to the eastern Mediterranean where traders faced the hazard of pirates. The *Rose Garden*, a Topsham barque laden with goods belonging to Exeter merchants, was captured and the crew carried off. Ships did not always need to sail that far away to be attacked as records show that Turkish pirates ventured into the Channel and captured a ship 'within three leagues of Dartmouth' at a cost of £5,000 to Exeter merchants.

four

The Civil War

In 1612 the rough ground below the city wall at Northernhay was levelled and planted to provide Exeter with the first public pleasure park in England.

Until 1637 Exonians could only be buried in the graveyard surrounding the cathedral. Burials had taken place here for a thousand years and as a result the ground level had risen considerably. As the cathedral authorities claimed the

Northernhay Gardens. The slope outside the city wall was first opened in 1612 as the first public park in England.

fee from each burial it is obvious why funerals were not permitted elsewhere within the city walls. There were now so many bodies buried within the Close that the decision was taken to close the yard for sixteen years and level and enclose the ground. A new cemetery was consecrated on 24 August 1637, St Bartholomew's Day, in the area known as Britayne. The graveyard became known as Bartholomew's Yard but was later to become the churchyard of Allhallows on the Wall. The graveyard continued to be used until the cholera epidemic of 1832.

Matthew Locke was one of the cathedral's most famous choristers. He was born in Exeter in 1630 and eight years later carved his name in the organ screen where it can still be seen. In later life Locke became court composer to Charles II.

When the Civil War between Charles I and his Parliament broke out in 1642 Exeter, like everywhere else, had its divisions. The dean and chapter of the cathedral were Royalist, as were the leading merchants, but the city chamber was for Parliament. As the war developed, a constant watch was maintained by thirty-two selected citizens against sudden attack, while supplies of food and ammunition were gathered together and stored in preparation for any situation which may arise. Six guns were mounted for the defence of the city.

During the winter of 1642 Parliamentarian sympathies within the city grew. Eventually all the Royalists were edged out of key positions within the city and Exeter prepared to come under attack from the forces of Sir Ralph Hopton who was attempting to secure the west of England for the King. After failing to capture Plymouth, Hopton turned his attention to Exeter, reaching the outskirts towards the end of the year. By now the city was well defended and when Hopton called for its surrender the mayor, Christopher Clark, refused. Dangerously short of supplies the Royalists decided against a prolonged action and withdrew.

Throughout the winter the city's defences were further strengthened. Extra protective ditches were dug around the perimeter to prevent enemy artillery from coming within close range of the walls, while outlying houses were demolished to widen the field of fire for the defenders and deny cover to attackers. Lookouts were posted on the church of St Mary Major and fire precautions undertaken.

Eventually, on 19 June 1643, a Royalist force under the command of Sir John Berkeley laid siege to the city. Across the river in Cowick Street the Royalists turned several buildings including the church, an inn, the prison and the manor house at Flowerpot fields, into strong points. On 31 July a band of 1,000 Roundheads sallied out from the West Gate, crossed Exe Bridge and attacked the besieging Royalists, driving them back from the river. Eighty Royalists were taken prisoner. During August Berkeley was reinforced by Prince Maurice, the King's nephew, and after eleven weeks Exeter surrendered on 4 September. Berkeley became governor and the city's Royalist officials were restored. A strong garrison was maintained and Exeter became the King's headquarters in the West.

Above: Houses on the original stone Exe Bridge.

Right: The Parliamentarians surrender to Prince Maurice and the garrison marches out, 1643.

As the main fighting of the Civil War shifted away, Queen Henrietta Maria moved to Exeter from threatened Oxford. She arrived on 1 May 1644 and stayed at Bedford House, the town house of the Earl of Bedford. It was here, on the morning of Sunday 16 June, that she gave birth to a daughter, Henrietta Anne. The Princess was christened in the cathedral by the Chancellor, Dr Lawrence Burnell. A new font was installed especially for the occasion but views differ as to whether it is the one that can be seen in the cathedral today.

Meanwhile Parliamentarian forces under the command of the Earl of Essex were again advancing into the West Country. By 5 July the Roundheads had reached Tiverton and with danger threatening once more the Queen, escorted by Prince Maurice, secretly left Exeter and made her way to Falmouth from where she left by ship for France. Henrietta Maria was forced to leave her new daughter in the care of the faithful Countess of Dalkeith, and it would be two years before mother and daughter were reunited in France.

However, the Royalist army with King Charles in the vanguard were in close pursuit of Essex. While the earl cut across country to Okehampton and then down into Cornwall, the King entered Exeter on 26 July accompanied by Charles, Prince of Wales. The loyal citizens presented the King with £500 and the Prince with £100 but after learning that the army was in need of new footwear the chamber gave a further £200 to buy 3,000 pairs of shoes. The royal party stayed at Bedford House where the King saw his daughter for the first and only time. The next day he knighted Mayor Hugh Crocker for his loyalty.

Charles wasted little time in continuing his pursuit of Essex finally bringing him to battle at Lostwithiel where a decisive action resulted in victory for the Royalists.

The King stopped at Exeter again on his way back, this time staying in the city for a week, before continuing his march to Oxford. A year later the Royalist army suffered a significant defeat by Parliament's New Model Army at the Battle of Naseby. This enabled Oliver Cromwell to send his general, Sir Thomas Fairfax, to subdue Royalist power in the west of England. Having captured Bristol, Fairfax marched into the South West taking Chard and then heading into Devon. But his plan to bottle up the Royalist forces in Devon and Cornwall failed when the majority of the King's cavalry managed, under cover of darkness, to slip pass his pickets in the lanes around Honiton. Having crossed the Devon border Fairfax gradually surrounded Exeter. Tiverton Castle fell to Fairfax in October and he moved his army down the Exe Valley to Silverton. Here Fairfax and his officers had to decide whether to press on and attack Exeter or to attempt to relieve Plymouth, which had been under siege for two years. The Roundheads could not risk marching west while leaving Exeter with its garrison of 1,000 cavalry and 8,000 infantry in their rear.

The decision was taken to closely besiege the city. Fairfax rode to Stoke Hill from where he was able to study the defences at close quarters. His army moved to Newton St Cyres with the intention of crossing the Whitestone hills to Alphington. But the wet weather and muddy lanes proved too much for the army's baggage train and the Parliamentarians were force to pull back to Crediton, where they were joined by Oliver Cromwell. Fairfax changed his plan and moved part of his force around the city to Topsham. Expecting an immediate attack the Royalist defenders in Exeter burnt some eighty houses outside the South Gate to improve their field of fire. The city was now totally blockaded from the east with outposts at Nutwell House on the river and at Broadclyst, Poltimore and Stoke Canon. In the west the Parliamentarians held Canonteign in Teign Valley and Sir George Chudley's house at Ashton.

On the evening of Sunday 14 December 1645 a force of 200 Roundheads under Captain Dean crossed the river from Nutwell, under cover of darkness, to attack Powderham Castle. Finding the castle's defences stronger than anticipated

Dean's small force withdrew to the church which they fortified. Provisions were ferried across to them and the next night soldiers from the castle, reinforced by 500 men sent down from Exeter, attacked the church. A bloody skirmish ensued with the Royalists throwing hand grenades into the barricaded strong point. The encounter lasted for three hours after which the Royalists withdrew. The Roundheads held out for two more days in bitterly cold weather before eventually pulling back across the river.

The final push against Exeter was delayed again in January while Cromwell attacked and captured Dartmouth, after which the garrison at Powderham Castle suddenly surrendered. Exeter was now cut off, but Fairfax's attack was delayed yet again when he received news that Royalist troops, commanded by Lord Goring, were heading for Barnstaple while others were approaching from Dorset. The Roundheads feared that these would join forces and attempt to relieve Exeter. The decision was made to storm Exeter and a call went out to commandeer every available ladder for miles around. The order went as far as Plymouth.

Meanwhile the Royalists had reached Torrington on their march to relieve Exeter. The city was now completely surrounded as Fairfax had established outposts at Alphington and at Barley House (much later the County Library headquarters) on the hillside above St Thomas. Any approach up the river was covered by the garrisons at Nutwell and now Powderham, as well as a fort at Exmouth.

The major part of Fairfax's army had marched to Torrington where Hopton's Royalist force was decisively defeated. At the height of the battle the parish church, which was packed with kegs of gunpowder and many prisoners, was deliberately blown up.

By the end of March with the Parliamentary army surrounding Exeter, the city's governor, Sir John Berkeley, realised his situation was hopeless, and, without a shot being fired, accepted Fairfax's call to surrender. Both parties met at Poltimore House, the home of Sir John Bampfylde, where terms were agreed. No plundering would be allowed and the little Princess Henrietta and her governess should be free to leave without hindrance. The Royalist garrison would retain all their equipment and march out with flags and banners flying. This they did on Monday 13 April.

The citizens were not so lucky. Many were fined heavily for supporting the Royalist cause. The Roundheads soon forgot the clause regarding plunder. Windows in the cathedral were smashed and statues frequently beheaded. The gates of the Close were torn down, clergy driven from the houses, and the chapter house used as stables, as was the Bishop's Palace.

Soldiers ripped out pipes from the organ and paraded through the streets 'piping in a scornful and contemptuous manner'. One group are said to have met some of the choristers whom they taunted by saying 'Boys we have spoilt your trade; you must go and sing hot pudding pies'.

For the next fourteen years the city would remain under military occupation. In January 1656 the chamber began negotiations with John Embree, the

The Bishop of Crediton's house in Cathedral Close.

surveyor of Cromwell's Office of Works to purchase the cathedral cloisters which they wished to use for a new cloth hall or serge market to replace the leaky old one in South Street. The cloisters were sold for £2,230 and the serge market built, probably along the east wall of the chapter house. Before building could begin parts of the damaged organ, which had been stored in the cloisters, were ordered to be melted down or disposed of. The new market opened on 30 October 1657.

Between 1657 and 1662 the cathedral was divided by a brick wall to allow different sects to use the building for worship at the same time. The two halves were known as East Peter's (used by the Presbyterians) and West Peter's (the Congregationalist Independents). Cromwell, now Lord Protector, designated his personal chaplain, Lewis Stukely, to be minister of West Peter's.

None of these changes would last long. With the restoration of the monarchy in 1660 a new youthful dean, Seth Ward, rapidly returned things to normal. The wall was torn down and the serge market closed and converted into a music school for the choristers and houses for the organist and two vergers. Another part of the market between the buttresses on the north side of the cloisters was converted into a hospital for distressed families.

In 1665 John Loosemore built a splendid new organ to replace the one damaged by the Puritans. Over the years virtually every part of Loosemore's instrument has been replaced or updated, but its magnificent carved timber case still dominates the screen between the nave and quire.

During the Commonwealth those who supported the restoration of the monarchy met at the Black Boy Inn on the Pinhoe Road outside the city. The name of the inn gave a clue to political leanings of its regulars as the swarthy features of Charles II had prompted his mother to call him 'my black boy'.

General Monk, one of those responsible for the restoration in 1660, had Exeter connections. His mother was the daughter of Sir George Smyth who was mayor in 1607. Charles rewarded Monk's loyalty by creating him Duke of Albemarle while the chamber granted him the Freedom of the City. On 11 May

The nave of the cathedral. The screen marked the dividing wall between East and West Peter during the Commonwealth. The great organ above it was built by John Loosemore in 1660 to replace the one destroyed by the Puritans.

1660 proclamations of the King's return were announced at the Guildhall, the Little Conduit in Cathedral Close, the Great Conduit and at St John's Bow. The conduits, as had been traditional on such occasions, flowed with claret.

Following the Restoration the city marked the anniversary of Charles I's execution at Whitehall on 30 January 1649 with an annual service at the cathedral. It became a solemn procession from the Guildhall. At the head of the procession, wrapped in black crepe, was carried the great sword presented by Edward IV. This practice continued until 1835 since when the mourning sword has only been carried at memorial services for members of the Royal Family or very prominent people. The last occasion was for Sir Winston Churchill in 1965.

Charles II paid a short visit to Exeter when, after visiting Plymouth to inspect the new Citadel, the royal yacht was becalmed at Dartmouth and the King decided to return to London overland. Charles arrived in Exeter on the evening of 23 July 1670 and stayed overnight at the deanery where he was sumptuously entertained at the expense of the city. He was also presented with £500 in gold and in return knighted the mayor, Benjamin Oliver. Charles made an early start the next morning leaving the deanery at three o'clock in the morning to continue this journey to Wilton House near Salisbury. Charles was accompanied by his illegitimate son, James, Duke of Monmouth, and the royal party travelled in four coaches escorted by servants on horseback. The King's early departure prevented the traditional hogshead of wine being emptied into the Great Conduit at the Carfoix.

City regalia.

The following year the King sent, as a gift to the city, a portrait of his sister Henrietta Anne. The Princess had grown up in poverty in France with her mother but eventually married Phillipe, Duke of Orleans, the brother of Louis XIV, the Sun King. She had been described as the 'Fairest in all Christendom' but died suddenly in 1670, probably from peritonitis. The portrait, presented by Charles II, can be seen in the Guildhall while the tragic Princess is also depicted in a mural in the High Street completed in 1991.

In Exeter the earthworks built during the Civil War were removed and Southernhay levelled, while the Trinity Green, now the site of the South Gate Hotel, was consecrated as a burial ground. On the other side of the city Northernhay was restored as a pleasure garden.

In 1676 the canal was extended to Topsham and the Quay doubled in length. The Custom House, Exeter's first brick building, was constructed in 1680.

That year James, Duke of Monmouth, visited Exeter as part of a West Country tour during which he sought support for his claim to succeed to his father's throne. He travelled with 500 horsemen and 900 young men in white uniforms. Monmouth was entertained at the deanery by Sir William Courtenay, but the chamber warily avoided having any contact with him and the cathedral bells did not ring.

Superstition and belief in witchcraft was still very much part of life in secluded Devonshire. At the summer assizes of 1682 three elderly women from Bideford were tried and convicted of witchcraft. The evidence against them was compounded by confessions obtained, as was normal at the time, under torture. The trio of supposed witches were hanged at Heavitree on 25 August.

Southernhay West.

The Custom House and the King's Chimney. The cannons which guard it were brought from the battlefield at Waterloo.

When Charles II died in February 1685 he was succeeded by his brother, James II. James was an unpopular heir both with Parliament and the majority of the people due to his public adoption of Catholicism. Monmouth, who had been exiled in Holland was persuaded to returned and claim the throne. He landed at Lyme Regis, quickly gathered an army of locals and was declared King at Taunton, but after failing to capture Bristol his peasant army was defeated outside Bridgwater at the Battle of Sedgemoor. King James' retribution was swift and merciless; the captured Monmouth was beheaded on Tower Hill, while many of his followers were sentenced to death by Judge Jeffreys at the Bloody Assizes. One of Jeffreys' Assizes opened at Exeter Guildhall on 14 September at which thirteen rebels were condemned to death. They were hanged, drawn and quartered then their boiled remains were distributed to twelve Devon towns to be displayed. Seven others were sentenced to be transported abroad, and thirteen others flogged or fined.

Religious disquiet grew and two years later seven bishops including Jonathan Trelawney, the Bishop of Bristol and future prelate of Exeter, were imprisoned for refusing to read out the King's Declaration of Indulgence. The Declaration suspended penal laws relating to ecclesiastical matters, allowed worship other than that of the established Church of England, and ended requirements for religious oaths before civic and military advancement. 20,000 Cornishmen set out to march to London, in the words of the well-known song, 'to know the reason why?' The march ended at Exeter where the protesters learned that the bishops had been released.

In June 1688 James married his second wife the Italian Catholic, Mary of Modena. Within days an invitation was sent by a group of prominent people, known as the Immortal Seven, and which included the Earl of Devon and the Bishop of London, to Prince William of Orange in Holland inviting him to invade England. William, a grandson of Charles I, was married to Princess Mary, the daughter of James II. The invitation assured William of military support should he undertake an invasion under the Protestant banner.

That autumn William sailed for England with fifty ships and 30,000 men. He evaded James' fleet, but instead of heading north for Hull and York he sailed safely down the Channel and landed on the beach at Brixham on 5 November. Once ashore William and his army marched inland via Newton Abbot.

William's first priority was to establish himself at Exeter from where he could assess the support for his cause. The Prince's army crossed Haldon in heavy rain and strong winds and William sent one of his officers, Captain Hicks, and a troop of cavalry ahead to Exeter.

Mol's Coffee House, one of Exeter's best-known landmarks.

Hicks found large numbers of men waiting to enlist under the Prince's protestant banner, but the city's leaders, clearly remembering Monmouth's failed cause, were extremely cautious. The mayor, Christopher Brodridge, promptly arrested Hicks when he refused to say on whose authority he was acting. The crowd that had gathered prevented Captain Hicks from being taken away, so he remained at the Guildhall guarded by two constables.

Later Lord Mordaunt and Dr Burnett, the Prince's chaplain, reached Exeter but found the West Gate closed. They commanded the porter to open it on pain of death. Once inside the city walls they demanded the release of Hicks and then ordered the mayor and magistrates to welcome the Prince of Orange on his arrival and govern the city for him. The mayor refused, saying that he had already sworn allegiance to the King. Meanwhile the bishop and dean had left the city, but the canons of the cathedral had remained behind. More of the Prince's troops arrived, crossing the ancient stone Exe Bridge and entering Exeter via the West Gate and then up the narrow Stepcote Hill. The next day, 9 November, the Prince himself reached Exeter from Powderham Castle, riding on a white charger and accompanied by the rest of his army.

Prince William took up residence in the deanery, and after taking some refreshment walked across to the cathedral where a solemn service was held. William sat in the bishop's throne, but the canons did not take their place in the stalls. When Dr Burnett read the Prince's proclamation and omitted to pray for King James the canons and choir hastily left the quire. So disappointed was the Prince with the attitude of the clergy and the civic powers that he threatened to return to his ships and sail back to Holland.

The reluctance of the city to welcome the Prince was without doubt due to the recent memories of the Bloody Assize, which made those in authority

West Street flanked by the 'house that moved' and St Mary Steps church with the Matthew the Miller clock.

extremely wary of changing sides too rapidly. Equally, concern for Exeter's position as England's most prosperous serge market and the possible loss of lucrative business would also have been a factor in the reluctance to switch allegiances too swiftly.

The momentum of William's advance was temporarily halted, but gradually, as an increasing number of influential lords came over to his side, the Prince's position grew in strength.

The dean, Richard Annesley, sent word begging forgiveness for having fled the city and requesting permission to visit him. The bishop, Thomas Lamplough, did not return. Instead he hurried to King James with news of the invasion and was rewarded by being appointed Archbishop of York.

The Prince of Orange remained in Exeter until 21 November, during which time numerous distinguished Devonians flocked to his standard; he then began his march to London. James meanwhile, as his army and advisers turned from him, abdicated and William and his consort Mary were invited to take the throne. Their coronation was celebrated in the traditional way by Exonians, as the conduits once again flowed with wine.

The population of Exeter in 1688 was 13,000 and the city ranked fourth or fifth in the land. Exeter had reached the zenith of its influence in the nation's history.

Below left: The West Gate, which was demolished in 1815.

Below right: Stepcote Hill – William of Orange's army entered the city up these steps.

five

Georgian Improvements

Exeter's serge trade was flourishing again by the turn of the century. Celia Fiennes who visited the city in 1698 was impressed with what she saw:

> Exeter is a town very well built. A vast trade is carried on …there is an incredible quantity of serges made and sold in the town. Their market day is Friday which supplies with all things like a fair almost. The market for meat, fowl, fish, garden things, and dairy produce takes up three whole streets, besides the large market house set on stone pillars which runs a great length, on which they lay their packs of serges. Just by it is another walk within pillars which is for yarn. The whole town and country is employed for at least twenty miles around in spinning, weaving, dressing and scouring, fulling and drying of serges. It turns the most money in a week of anything in England.

Daniel Defoe was another traveller to be impressed by Exeter's serge industry. He visited the city in 1714 and was surprised to find that, 'Tis full of gentry and good company, and yet full of trade and manufactures also'. He continued, 'The serge market held here every week is very well worth a stranger seeing, and next to the Briggs Market at Leeds in Yorkshire, is the greatest in England.'

Defoe also reported that the canal had been extended all the way to Topsham and was wide and deep enough to allow ships to be unloaded at the Quay. As

Exeter from the canal.

well as the woollen trade being plied with Holland, wine was being imported from Portugal, Spain and Italy.

Exeter had also become the third city in England to have a newspaper. Farley's *Exeter Post Man* is believed to have been launched in 1704. Joseph Bliss' *Exeter Post Boy* followed in 1707 and seven years later the *Exeter Mercury* was launched.

A notable figure in Exeter's early newspaper industry was Andrew Brice. He was apprenticed to Bliss but ran away. At the age of twenty-five Brice created his own paper *The Post Master* which got him into trouble with the House of Commons for breach of privilege. In 1725 he published *Brice's Weekly Journal* and his writings have provided much information on Georgian Exeter.

Twenty-year-old John Baring arrived at Exeter from Bremen in Germany in 1717. He came to learn the woollen trade and was apprenticed to Edmund Cook. Having become a fully-fledged serge maker Baring married the only daughter of John Vowler, a successful grocer, and himself became an equally successful cloth merchant. Indeed, when he died in 1748, Baring had become the city's most eminent businessman with a factory at Larkbeare. His sons John and Francis continued the family tradition, developing a wool import business in London as an extension of their Exeter ventures. In 1770 John Baring purchased the manor of Heavitree, and soon owned much of St Leonard's parish. He converted the Elizabethan house at Mount Radford into a Georgian mansion and the same year established the Devonshire Bank. His brother Francis became a merchant banker in London and it was said that the Baring brothers played a major role in financing the British Empire. With John's death in 1816 the Baring association with Exeter virtually ended and their estate was sold off in the 1820s. Much of it was bought by William Hooper, the builder. The mansion at Mount Radford later became a school and was demolished to make way for the development of Barnardo Road in 1902. The playing field of the Royal School for the Deaf is on the site of the mansion's lawn. Barings Bank survived until 1995 when it was brought down by the activities of rogue trader Nick Leeson. By then Barings was Britain's oldest merchant bank.

The leat re-enters the Exe at the Quay above the fish market.

John Wesley virtually founded Methodism in Exeter in 1739. He and his brother Charles had travelled to Devon to comfort the widow of another brother, Samuel, who had been headmaster of Blundell's School at Tiverton.

John was asked to preach at St Mary Arches church on Sunday 24 November 1739. His sermon made such an impact that the rector, although acknowledging that there was no fault with his doctrines, asked him not to return for the afternoon service as he feared that Wesley's nonconformist concepts were dangerous and liable to cause 'enthusiasm'. There was clearly room for 'enthusiasm' within the Church of England at that time. Andrew Brice had observed 'sleepy maids sent to early service at the cathedral for the good of their lie-abed mistresses' souls'.

Charles Wesley returned to Exeter in 1743 and preached an open-air sermon to around 1,000 people. The congregation was made up in the main of 'gentlemen and ladies with some clergy'.

Exeter's first theatre opened in Waterbeer Street around 1750. Prior to that in the early 1700s performances had been given in an upstairs room or sometimes in summer in the garden alongside the river at the Seven Stars Inn on the corner of Okehampton Street and Cowick Street in St Thomas. Here *The Beggar's Opera* was staged for what was believed to be the first time outside London. The Seven Stars survived until the late 1930s when it was partly demolished to make way for road improvements. The work was delayed and the Luftwaffe finished the job a few years later.

The first purpose-built theatre was located in Waterbeer Street. This thoroughfare, which no longer exists, ran from North Street along the rear of High Street to Goldsmith Street. The theatre may possibly have been built by the Bath Players with support from Andrew Brice, the printer and newspaper man. To overcome licensing problems Brice sold packets of tooth powder which doubled as theatre tickets, whereby the theatre proprietors were not seen to be charging admission.

Following John Wesley's open-air sermon the theatre was taken over by the Methodists as a chapel. Once again Brice and his associates may have come to the actors' aid using some questionable methods. The *London Morning Post* of 16 May 1745 reported that:

> In Exeter, the Methodists had a meeting house behind the Guildhall, and on 6 May the mob gathered at the door and pelted those who entered with potatoes, mud and dung. On coming out, the congregation were all beaten, without exception; many were trampled under foot; many fled without their hats and wigs.

The mob's tactics eventually paid off and the actors regained their theatre which remained in use until 1787. The Methodists bravely struggled on in Exeter but unsurprisingly their sect did not flourish and towards the end of the century they numbered just twenty-six. It was not until 1810 that interest for Methodism began to increase and by 1815 their numbers had grown to 300.

From 1750 onwards changes began to be made to the medieval city. Transport access in and out of the city required improvement. The main route into Exeter from the west was via the medieval Exe Bridge then through the West Gate and up the steep and narrow Stepcote Hill. This was alleviated when a new three arch bridge across the Exe was opened to traffic in 1778. The new bridge, designed by Joseph Dixon, was sited further upstream, so was able to be linked through a recently demolished gap in the city wall to New Bridge Street which crossed the leats on Exe Island via three arches and then joined Fore Street, from which soil had been removed from the top the hill to ease the incline both at the top and the bottom. Construction of the bridge was delayed when on 18 January 1775 a great flood 'entirely destroyed the foundations and carried away all the arches of the new bridge and greatly terrified the neighbouring inhabitants lest it should damage the old bridge'.

Above: New Bridge Street was created in 1778 to carry traffic from the second Exe Bridge.

Left: The North Gate, the first gate to be removed in 1769.

Further bottlenecks were eased when the main city gates were demolished over a period of fifty years. The first, the North Gate, was torn down in 1769 followed by the East Gate in 1784 thus allowing coaches and wagons to enter the High Street without delay. The West Gate was demolished in 1815 and finally the historic South Gate four years later. The Great Conduit, which was a source of water for a large part of the population, was removed from the junction of South Street, North Street and High Street to allow carts to pass in 1780. There was no public outcry at the removal of these historic landmarks, indeed the demolitions seemed to have been popular. The South Gate, which had seen the entry of many historical figures starting with William the Conqueror, was also infamous as the city prison. The conditions within the two great towers where the prisoners were incarcerated were notoriously bad. The room above the main gateway was known as 'the Shoe' and housed debtors. The inmates here had to depend on friends and relatives for their source of food or were forced to beg from passers-by. To do this a shoe was lowered down to street level into which benefactors could place their alms. From this necessity comes the expression 'living on a shoe string'.

Below left: The South Gate showing debtors lowering a shoe for alms.

Below right: The plaque marking the site of the South Gate.

When the South Gate was demolished in 1819 along with the adjoining Trinity church the prisoners were transferred to the newly-built City Prison. In 1863 this too was closed and the inmates transferred to the County Gaol. The prison was demolished and replaced by the Rougemont Hotel.

The County Gaol had been built in 1790. The opening of the new gaol ended another tradition, that of public hangings on the gallows at Heavitree. Condemned felons now met their end on the 'new drop' scaffold above the prison gatehouse. Executions took place at midday and crowds flocked into the city to watch from the Longbrook valley.

Not far from the new gaol a new cavalry barracks had already been built. Many of the British Army's most famous regiments would be billeted here including the Inniskilling Dragoons and Scots Greys. Exonians regularly strolled across the Longbrook valley in the evening to listen to the music of the regimental bands.

Another significant development for the city was the establishment of the Devon and Exeter Hospital in 1741. The hospital was the brainchild of the newly appointed dean of the cathedral, Dr Alured Clarke.

Until the dissolution of the monasteries under Henry VIII in the 1540s the sick had been treated and cared for by the monks. Thereafter for the next 200 years there was no medical provision for the poor, while the better off were able to pay for a doctor.

Dr Clarke was appointed to Exeter in January 1741 having previously been Dean of Winchester. At Winchester he had established a voluntary hospital and on his arrival in Exeter wasted little time in setting up a similar facility. Indeed he moved so quickly that the hospital received its first patients a year later. His idea was launched at a meeting in the cathedral chapter house on 23 July 1741. The initial requirement was £3,000 and this sum was raised by Clarke sending an appeal to every church and chapel appealing for donations. Each contributing body or individual would be entitled to nominate one patient for treatment. The site in Southernhay, then in open country outside the city wall, was offered by future MP John Tuckfield. The plans were drawn up in three weeks and the foundation stone laid shortly after. The builder, John Richards, gave his services

The Royal Devon and Exeter Hospital, built in 1742-43.

free of charge, while several local landowners donated the building materials. The speed of the development and construction of Dean Clarke's project was staggering by today's standards. Perhaps that was fortunate as the good dean sadly died at the age of forty-six on 3 May 1742, just seventeen months after arriving in Exeter. He was buried in Westminster Abbey.

The hospital received its first patients on 1 January 1742. Patients were admitted on Thursdays and had the rules read to them the next morning. While in hospital those patients who were fit enough were required to help the staff look after the other patients. The strongest ones also had to take turns pumping water from the well to the cistern in the roof. This system continued until 1815 when the hospital was connected to the main supply.

In 1748 a north wing was added, followed eight years later by an operating theatre, surgical ward and casualty department.

The hospital served the city for 250 years. It became the Royal Devon and Exeter in 1899, the Royal title being bestowed by Queen Victoria after the Duke and Duchess of York, later George V and Queen Mary, had named a new ward 'Victoria' during their visit that year. Having withstood the air raids of 1942 and a serious fire in 1967 it was replaced by a modern development on a site at Barrack Road in 1974. The original building, now named Dean Clarke House, houses the local health authority offices.

Georgian Exeter remained an unsanitary place. The city still lacked sewers and ordure was thrown into the street while the livestock markets continued to be held in the High Street. Heavy rain was welcomed to wash the streets, but disease was rife. In 1775 the chamber ended the use of the Snayle Tower on the western wall below Bartholomew Yard as a public latrine, setting up an alternative in the fields below, while records show that the populace continued to use the wall of St Lawrence church in High Street as a urinal.

For centuries the city had been a dark place at night but by 1768 it boasted 168 streetlights. Ten years later pavements were added to the main streets but the first sewers were not constructed until 1807.

It was during this period of improvement that some of Exeter's finest buildings were constructed. William Mackworth Praed built his Assembly Rooms in Cathedral Close in 1768. Two years later this building had become known as 'the hotel', the first such establishment in England, after being taken over by the Frenchman Peter Berlon, and in 1827 it became the Royal Clarence Hotel after the Duchess of Clarence, wife of the future William IV, stayed there.

Adjoining the Assembly Rooms was the Exeter Bank, the first of several finance houses to be established on the profits from the woollen trade. A year later John Baring set up the Devonshire Bank, which was followed first by the City Bank, adjacent to Broadgate, then General Bank in 1792, and the Western Bank a year later.

Mr Robert Stribling began construction of Bedford Circus in 1773 with 'fourteen genteel houses' built on the site of Bedford House. Although planned as a circular development, the houses on the southern side were not completed until around 1826. Sadly this beautiful example of old Exeter was destroyed by

The Royal Clarence Hotel.

Rougemont House.

incendiary bombs during the 1942 Blitz and shortly afterwards the burnt-out shell was knocked down as the remaining structure was deemed unsafe. This has long been a bone of contention among Exonians, many of whom believe that the Circus could have been restored.

Another well-known Exeter establishment was founded around 1789 when a war widow, Mrs Colson went into business as a 'linen draper, haberdasher, milliner and tea dealer'. Mrs Colson's enterprise would become one of the best-known shops in Exeter and is still flourishing today, although now it is known as Dingles and is part of the House of Fraser group.

George III visited Exeter in 1789. The King had recently recovered from one of his periodic bouts of illness and was travelling through the West Country in the company of Queen Charlotte and their daughters, Charlotte, the Princess Royal, Augusta and Elizabeth. The royal party had travelled from Windsor by way of Salisbury and Weymouth. Before reaching Exeter at 7.00 p.m. on Thursday 13 August their majesties had taken 'an elegant and sumptuous repast' at Escot House on the Honiton Road. Upon their arrival in the city the royal party was met at the bottom of Paris Street by a party of constables and conducted to the site of the East Gate (the historic gate having been demolished five years earlier) where the mayor, Jonathan Burnett, the chamber and members of the trade corporations, in livery, waited to greet them. Two hundred respectable tradesmen had been sworn in as special constables to control the huge crowds, estimated at 40,000, and crush barriers were set up in High Street, where the main drain had been boarded over and gravelled especially for the occasion.

The procession made its way to the deanery where the royal party would stay, greeted by all the church bells ringing out a welcome. During the evening the city was fully illuminated while the people celebrated with fireworks and bonfires. At the deanery the King and his family were guarded by the Inniskilling Dragoons, who were stationed in the city at the new cavalry barracks.

Below top: A procession of the Sheriff's Javelin Men along High Street to meet the judges.

Below: A civic procession to the cathedral passes through Broadgate.

The following morning the mayor and chamber were presented to King George at the deanery where the recorder proffered a civic address which greatly pleased the Queen. Later in the morning the royal party took the short walk to the cathedral where they were met by Bishop John Ross who conducted them to their seats in the quire. The King and Queen sat in the bishop's throne while the three princesses sat opposite below the pulpit. The cathedral was packed for the service which was attended by all the local clergy, civic dignitaries and trade corporations preceded by their beadles carrying their staffs of office.

Following the service the King held a levee at the Bishop's Palace, the first to be held since his illness, and later the royal party walked in the garden and appeared on the wall walk where they could be seen by thousands of excited onlookers.

That evening the royal visit took on an element of farce. The chamber had intended to entertain the King to a lavish banquet at the Guildhall but Dean Butler who was said to have conceived the royal visit as a personal compliment to himself and his wife, prevented the invitation reaching his majesty. Instead he and the bishop took the King on a private tour of the cathedral. The chamber had spent a considerable amount of money, £437 (the equivalent of £40,000 in today's money) including £130 for transparencies and illuminations, on preparing the banquet while Alderman Dennis had personally spent £24 on refurbishing the uniforms of the city band for the occasion.

When the King did not appear at the Guildhall the enraged alderman managed to get inside the closed cathedral and attempted to confront the King. However, Dean Buller spotted Dennis approaching and tried to head him off. A heated argument ensued with the situation becoming reminiscent of Anthony Trollope's 'Barchester Chronicles' novels. The Dean remained adamant and eventually the alderman was evicted by the vergers. The truth of the matter was that the King probably did not wish to set a precedent whereby he would have to attend similar functions at every provincial town he visited.

The following morning the royal party took their leave of the city and continued their tour, going on to Saltram House near Plymouth. The return journey saw them make another overnight stay at the deanery.

The deanery. Catherine of Aragon, the Prince of Orange, and George III all stayed here.

Among those accompanying the King and Queen was the novelist Fanny Burney who wrote that she found Exeter 'close and ugly'.

The royal visit was also the subject of a long satirical and amusing poem written in Devonshire dialect by Dr John Wolcot under the pen name of Peter Pindar.

Exeter at the turn of the nineteenth century was a dirty and smelly place but the Mayor Thomas Floud tried to do something about the problem by introducing a by-law which required Exonians to sweep in front of their houses three times a week. Floud also attempted to get street names displayed for the first time, the names being painted on street corners.

Exeter's woollen industry had declined sharply in the later half of the eighteenth century and was unable to match the growing industrial might of the Midlands and the North. The Napoleonic Wars speeded the decline of trade even further in that the naval blockade of the European ports meant that the city's merchants could not export their wares for its duration. The other side of the coin was that while the country gentry still came to town to attend the concerts, balls and military ceremonials, which took place during the Assizes and elections, Exeter also developed a tourist trade as foreign travel was impractical for twenty years, and the new wealthy middle class were attracted to the city thanks to its pleasant location and climate. The arrival of these affluent families triggered a building boom both within the city and in the surrounding suburbs of St Leonard's and Heavitree. Between 1800 and 1840 the population of Exeter doubled from 20,000 to 40,000.

Exeter's most famous builders, William Hooper and Matthew Nosworthy, were busy during this period. Nosworthy was responsible for Colleton Crescent, Dix's Field, Barnfield Crescent and much of Southernhay, while Hooper built Higher and Lower Summerlands, Baring Place, Chichester Place in Southernhay and much of St Leonard's using land purchased from the Baring family. John Brown built Pennsylvania Park for Joseph Sparkes, the Quaker and partner in the General Bank. This magnificent terrace of six houses with its stunning view of the Exe estuary was named in honour the American William Penn and eventually gave its name to the whole area.

Colleton Crescent stands
above the Quay.

Higher Summerlands in Heavitree Road, built by William Hooper in 1804 and destroyed in 1942, now the site of the police station.

A new theatre had been built by Richard Hughes, the owner of the previous Waterbeer Street theatre, at the entrance to Bedford Circus from Southernhay in 1787. It stood on the site now occupied by Fanum House, the former AA office. When Fanum House was built in the early sixties its design reflected that of the 'New Theatre' which had preceded it. Sarah Siddons appeared here as did Edmund Keen, but in 1820 it was destroyed by fire due to a fault in the gas lighting fitted three years previously. Within twelve months the theatre was rebuilt. Sadly it too was badly damaged by fire. Its shell was again rebuilt, this time as a drill hall. Like so many of Exeter's historic buildings it was destroyed by enemy action in May 1942.

The French Wars meant that Exeter again became a garrison town, with its close proximity to the coast and naval connections, including Captain Thomas Louis of HMS *Minotaur*. Louis, a native of Exeter, won Nelson's respect by giving him close support at a critical stage of the Battle of the Nile in 1798 which also earned him the Freedom of the City. Nelson too received a sword from the chamber in recognition of his victory.

At the other end of the naval spectrum was Richard Parker, the son of a baker from the parish of St Mary Major. Parker led the mutiny at the Nore as a result of which he was hanged.

The officers from cavalry barracks were welcomed in Exeter society by hostesses and tradesmen alike. Not only did the officers require uniforms, transport and accommodation but they also made an attractive addition at dinner tables and social gatherings through the city. In return the military hosted balls and galas, while the city also enjoyed military ceremonial parades and band concerts. When the word reached Exeter that the Scots Greys were to be stationed at the Barracks the city's dancing masters were reported to have 'perfected themselves in the different Scotch dances'.

1 A passageway leading to Cathedral Close. Prior to the 1942 Blitz, Exeter had many alleys and
courtyards. This picture is one of a series of postcards issued by Worth & Co. in the early twentieth
century. Worth's had a shop in Mol's Coffee House in Cathedral Close.

2 The Bishop's Palace dates from the thirteenth century. This picture shows the bay window added by Bishop Phillpotts in 1845. Behind the Palace towers the cathedral, and to the left of the tree can be seen the Chapter House.

3 Exeter Ship Canal was a popular subject for artists. This nineteenth-century view offers an idea of the amount of shipping that once used the Quay.

4 West Street and the church of St Mary Steps. The entrance to Stepcote Hill is hidden between the church and the medieval shops in the foreground.

5 Exeter's Guildhall dates from around 1160. The portico with its granite pillars and the Mayor's Parlour above were added in 1592.

6 The city wall is still much in evidence, as seen here on Quay Hill behind the Georgian Customs House.

7 The stretch of city wall leading up from the Quay towards the site of the South Gate.

8 The Royal Devon and Exeter Hospital was built in 1742, it received its first patients early the following year and its last in 1974. The Royal prefix was bestowed by Queen Victoria in 1899. Now named Dean Clarke House after its founder, the building currently houses the offices of the local health authority.

9 above left The seventeenth-century weathervane once again stands above the site of the West Gate.

10 above right A quiet Exeter backwater close to the city centre.

11 Stepcote Hill was once the main thoroughfare into the city from the west. William of Orange and his army rode up here on their arrival at Exeter in 1688.

12 Bartholomew Yard was consecrated as a cemetery on 24 August 1637 when it was decided that the Cathedral Yard had reached its capacity. Exonians were buried here for the next 200 years, the last burial taking place during the cholera epidemic of 1832.

13 The 'house that moved' now stands close to the site of the West Gate. The medieval house, dating from 1430, was moved from its original location in Frog Street several hundred yards up the hill to facilitate the construction of Western Way in 1961.

14 The first stone bridge across the Exe was built by Nicholas Gervase and his son, Walter, around 1190. The bridge was in use until 1775 and several arches still remain.

15 St Martin's church and Mol's Coffee House. The design of the coffee house bears a resemblance to the stern of a Tudor warship, and it was a regular meeting place for Queen Elizabeth I's sea captains, including Sir Francis Drake.

16 Southernhay was once the scene of gruesome executions before its fine terraced houses were built between 1798 and 1820. They were constructed by Matthew Nosworthy, one of the city's leading Georgian builders.

17 above Richard Hooker's statue sits in the snow on the Cathedral Green. Known as 'Judicious Hooker', he was born in Heavitree around 1553 and became a prominent theological writer during the reign of Elizabeth I.

18 right A deserted and snowy Queen Street in the 1980s. C&A's controversial building is on the right with the Marks and Spencer store under construction on the left. Queen Street was built across the Longbrook Valley. Work started in 1835 and was completed two years later in time for Queen Victoria's Coronation.

19 above A new housing development on Haven Banks Road.

20 opposite A lamp from the 1905 Exe Bridge now adorns the Quay. The bridge, which was built to carry the electric trams, was demolished in the early 1970s. The arches built into the cliff on the far bank of the river were the scene of a major oil fire in 1882. The historic Butt's Ferry can be seen to the right. Manipulated by hand along a wire stretched across the river, it has carried Exonians across the river since at least 1750.

21 Dutch influence on the Quay. Exeter's links with Holland through the serge trade is reflected in the architecture of this shop. The ships which sailed from the Quay often returned carrying bricks as ballast.

22 above The Victorian Higher Market,
designed by Charles Fowler and built by William
Hooper in 1838, was incorporated into the
design of the modern Guildhall shopping centre
which opened in 1975.

23 right Shops now line the old Victorian
Higher Market hall.

24 A sunny Sunday afternoon on the riverside at the Quay. This once busy industrial and trading area is now a popular leisure spot with Exonians and visitors alike.

Volunteer units were also raised to meet the threat of invasion. The Fencibles were the Napoleonic version of the Home Guard, and served alongside the militia, who were the equivalent of the later Territorial Army. The Yeomanry were cavalry units raised by local gentry from country gentlemen and farmers who could provide their own horses.

These volunteers had agreed only to serve at home. The fear that the growing spirit of revolution would spread across the Channel meant that the odds against these volunteers actually facing the French army were less than those turning their muskets on hungry fellow countrymen. While England was gripped with a patriotic fervour for the war, food prices were rising, hunger was growing and businesses were in difficulty. By 1796 Napoleon Bonaparte's armies controlled most of the European mainland, and that year they marched into Leghorn in Italy, Exeter's great trading partner in the Mediterranean. City merchants were reputed to have suffered losses amounting to £100,000.

While the volunteers may have been confident enough to face invading French soldiers should the case have arisen, many were more concerned with the possibility of having to turn their muskets on fellow Englishmen.

Food prices began to rise in 1760 as a result of several bad harvests and as wages did not increase to match the cost of living hardship was inevitable. The decline in the cloth trade meant that there was also increasing unemployment. The country landlords often helped to relieve the situation but bluntly refused to increase wages, which in many cases had remained static for more than fifty years. The poor believed that greedy millers were to blame and in the spring of 1796 stormed a corn mill at Chudleigh. The military managed to intervene and in

Mr John Cook, Captain of the Javelin Men.

the ensuing melee a blacksmith was seized. The unfortunate smith was made the scapegoat and was sentenced to death as an example to the populace. Feeling ran high in his favour in Exeter and on the day that he was due to be executed the authorities had a battalion of militia and two cannons standing by following rumours of a rescue attempt. In fact the hanging went ahead without hindrance.

Other incidents also took place at this time. Magistrates and constables were stoned in St Sidwell's and when the rioters were arrested the constables had to repel attempts to break them out of the Guildhall. Corn was plundered from a ship moored at Topsham Quay and sold at what the protesters considered a fair price.

Fortunately two good harvests helped to restore peace. Fears of revolution were certainly not unique to Exeter. Compared to some towns and cities Exeter's disturbances were very low key. William Pitt himself commented that 'big towns were heavily garrisoned, not against the French but against the hungry poor at home.' When Napoleon abdicated in 1814 a celebration dinner was laid on for 8,000 of Exeter's 'deserving poor persons.'

The war with France saw a second military barracks built in Exeter. In 1804 the Ordnance Board purchased eight acres of land from Mrs Alice Templer of the Old Abbey, Salmonpool, for £2,000 on which it planned to build an 'Artillery Barracks' to hold one company of foot artillery.

Artillery companies were named after their commanding officer and the first to be stationed at the new barracks in 1804 was Brome's Company. Five of the companies to be stationed there over the next eleven years distinguished themselves against the French. Curry's, Raynsford's and Lawson's fought in the Peninsula, while Brome's and Lloyd's Companies saw action at the Battle of Waterloo in 1815, where Captain Brome was killed.

By 1830 the Exeter woollen industry was finally dead and the city's position as a social and cultural capital came to an end. What had a century before been one of England's busiest trading ports now just handled coastal traffic.

The Guildhall, c. 1900.

six

Victorian Exeter

Queen Victoria would only pass through Exeter twice during her lifetime and it was reputed that for some reason she did not like the city. However, her reign saw Exeter undergo many changes. As an infant Victoria stayed at Sidmouth with her parents, the Duke and Duchess of Kent. The Duke died there on 23 January 1820, just before he was due to receive the Freedom of the City of Exeter. His body was brought to the Royal Clarence Hotel, where it was embalmed – in the kitchen, according to popular legend – before being removed to Windsor for burial.

Thirteen years later the young Victoria was greeted by the Mayor Henry Blackwell and the city council, as she and her mother sat in their coach, which had paused to change horses outside the New London Inn en route to Salcombe.

It would be another twenty-three years before she would be seen again, this time as Queen. By that time the railway had become part of Exeter life and the Royal Train stopped at St David's, en route from Plymouth to Osborne House on the Isle of Wight. The Queen is reported to have remained on board the train where she was addressed by the town clerk and presented with nosegays, fruit and refreshments by the mayor and council. In recognition of the occasion the station was carpeted and decorated with an abundance of flowers and flags.

The Victorian warehouses which became world famous as the location for the BBC drama *The Onedin Line*.

Victoria's accession to the throne came a mere five years after the 1832 Reform Bill had brought significant changes to Exeter's local government. The city's long established, self-elected ruling chamber was replaced by a city council or corporation elected by the citizens. John Gidley became the first town clerk and elections to the new council took place in December 1835. The Conservatives won by 3,232 votes to the Liberals 2,309. It was agreed that eighteen councillors would represent each of the two parties. One of the new Liberal councillors, John Dymond, was a Quaker, and his beliefs prevented him from taking the oath of office. He was therefore ineligible to serve which immediately gave the Conservative group a majority of one. This allowed Samuel Kingdom, known locally as 'Iron Sam', to take the chair, a situation which was exploited to the full as his party promptly elected five of their own councillors as aldermen to the Liberals' one – the former mayor, William Kellaway. This would set the balance of power for the foreseeable future as the Conservatives would retain their majority for the next sixty years. The situation would also prevent Mark Kennaway, a solicitor who was the city's leading Liberal and a member of the prominent banking family, from ever achieving the mayoralty. It also later prompted the eminent local historian W.G. Hoskin to remark that the moral of the story was that no one should 'trust any party politician of any colour. Children cannot learn this lesson too soon in life'.

The new council also found itself managing a massive debt thanks to an ill-advised scheme, supported by the engineer Thomas Telford, to carry out expensive improvements to the canal. In 1827 the canal had been extended two miles to enter the estuary at Turf while at the other end a new city basin had been opened in 1830. Bands, cannon fire and a procession of decorated barges had heralded the return of 'the commerce of the world' but the new development would become almost immediately outdated as canals were about to be superseded by the new railway age. The chamber thus found itself saddled with a £95,000 debt. A planned further extension of the canal to Crediton was actually begun but the workings around Exwick were later filled in.

The opening of the city basin.

In parliamentary elections Exeter returned two members, who frequently proved to be one from each party, a Liberal and a Conservative. In 1885 the city's representation was reduced to a single member who for the next twenty-two years would be a Conservative, although with an overall majority of only a few hundred votes.

One of the new council's major priorities would be to improve the hygiene in the city. In 1832 Exeter suffered a major cholera epidemic. The disease, unknown in Europe until this time, had swept through Germany and across the North Sea to Gateshead and Sunderland where the first case was reported in the autumn of 1831. From the North East it was carried south, probably by coastal shipping, reaching Plymouth in July 1832. The inhabitants of Exeter lived in fear of the disease and while sanitation and water supply still left much to be desired stringent quarantine precautions were put into operation at the Quay. A ship, *The Ranger*, arrived at the Quay from London on 19 July and its captain, Master Woofe, reported that one of his crew had died of cholera on the voyage. *The Ranger* was immediately quarantined. The same day the first case was reported in Exeter, a woman called Ruse in North Street, recently arrived from Plymouth, who died within a few hours. In St Thomas a stranger from London also died. Both victims were attended by Dr Thomas Shapter, from the Devon and Exeter Hospital, who would become one of the heroes of the epidemic and later wrote a graphic account of events.

The death rate gradually increased, going from three or four a day to eleven on 3 August and peeking to thirty deaths five days later. With so many funerals the burial grounds at Bartholomew's Yard and Trinity Yard had to be closed and alternative sites found. The council decided to procure Bury Meadow opposite St David's church, but local residents objected strongly and rioted at the first burial. The gravedigger was assaulted and his tools broken. It was discovered that the meadow had not been legally constituted as a burial ground and the funeral was transferred back early the following morning to Bartholomew Yard. The cortège was followed by an angry mob that strongly objected to the coffin

Bartholomew Yard, the last resting place of many Exonians.

being carried underarm due to the undertaker's men probably not wishing to risk infection. This was considered extremely disrespectful and as a result the Corporation of the Poor agreed to provide a hearse. Such was the death rate that a second hearse had to be acquired. A burial site for cholera victims in St Sidwell's parish was opened in Pennsylvania off Pester Lane, later to become known as Union Road.

From July until mid-October 402 people died in Exeter, while across the river in St Thomas a further thirty-eight expired. A large proportion of the victims came from the unsanitary slums of the West Quarter. Here, where once the rich merchants had lived, the old houses had been turned into tenements, with most properties housing several families living in appalling poverty amid piles of rotting filth with no running water or adequate sanitation. Large numbers of pigs were still kept within the city while poultry was housed in cellars and outhouses.

The medical profession worked valiantly to halt the epidemic and were held in high esteem, but not so Henry Philpotts, the new Bishop of Exeter, who quickly left his Palace and stayed away from the city throughout the duration of the epidemic. The Assizes continued without hindrance but although the theatre remained open it was noted the play 'William Tell' was performed to a 'beggarly account of empty boxes'.

In an attempt to stop the spread of inflection bodies were buried in lime while the clothes of the victims were burnt at the Shilhay and Lions Holt. However the smoke from the fires drifted over the city and instructions were issued that the clothes be buried instead. Later, this practice was also stopped and the garments washed in the river and reused. Consequently the city's drinking water was pumped in from a new works higher up the Exe at Pynes Mill while a reservoir was constructed at Danes Castle.

One of the medical heroes of the cholera epidemic was Dr Peter Hennis, who was also destined to become the last man in England to be killed in a duel. Dr Hennis was 'called out' by Sir John Jeffcott, a high court judge. The judge, who was about to take up a new post in Sierra Leone had spent an evening drinking

The Shilhay from Exe Bridge.

with friends at the Royal Clarence Hotel. One of his friends related gossip which implied Dr Hennis had spread rumours which were responsible for the break up of the judge's relationship with a young lady, a relative of Flora McDonald. By chance Hennis walked past the hotel entrance as the judge was leaving. A violent argument ensued as a result of which both men believed that they had been insulted by the other and a challenge was issued. The duel took place on Haldon racecourse at 3.30 in the afternoon. The duellists, armed with pistols, faced each other at fourteen paces; the command 'Prepare' was given, but before the order to 'Fire' could be made, Jeffcott shot and wounded Hennis. The judge left straight away for Plymouth from where he immediately sailed to Sierra Leone, but Hennis, severely wounded, was taken back to Exeter where he died eight days later. He was buried in St Sidwell's churchyard. In 2003 funds were raised to restore his grave which had been vandalised.

In the aftermath of the cholera epidemic sweeping changes were made to the city. £1,000 was spent on covering drains and washing the streets. Attempts were made to improve ventilation by opening up covered archways and courts, while street widening resulted in many medieval façades being replaced by Victorian shop frontages. A new main thoroughfare, connecting High Street with St David's, became known as Queen Street in honour of Victoria's coronation.

As part of the hygiene improvements two new markets were built. The Lower Market replaced the Shambles and Butchers Row where traditionally animals were slaughtered in the street before being butchered and the meat sold on stalls. The Higher Market, designed by Exeter-born architect Charles Fowler, was built in Queen Street by the Hooper brothers. Although this facility closed as a market in the 1960s its elegant and impressive façades were successfully incorporated in the new Guildhall Shopping Centre constructed in the mid-1970s. The cattle market was moved outside the city walls to a new site off Exe Island in Bonhay Road.

The Iron Bridge was built across the Longbrook Valley in 1835. This considerably eased entry into the city for horse-drawn vehicles and pack trains from north Devon. The bridge was manufactured in sections at a foundry at

The Higher Market, built in the 1830s. The façade was preserved and now fronts the Guildhall Shopping Centre. Queen Victoria's statue can be seen on top of the Marks and Spencer store next door.

Left: The Iron Bridge.

Below: The ironwork which gives the bridge its name was brought in sections from Wales.

Blaina in Wales and brought to Exeter by ship. Although the climb up the extremely narrow North Street was still very steep the new bridge cut out the sharp descent into the valley and the section up to the site of the old North Gate. Two years earlier a stone viaduct had been built across the Shute Valley at Bull Meadow, which helped to level the road in from Heavitree.

These improvements were necessary as, until the coming for the railway, all transport in and out of the city was horse-drawn. In 1831 forty-four coaches left Exeter on three days of the week while on the remaining three the number was thirty-three. Naturally no coaches ran on Sundays. The coaches travelled west to the seaports of Plymouth and Falmouth or north and east to London, Bristol, Bath, Brighton and Birmingham. The coaching trade centred around the New London Inn situated just outside the site of the East Gate. The Royal Mail coach left at 9.45 a.m. for London each morning and reached the capital at 6.30 a.m. the following day.

The coaching industry in Exeter employed some 125 men. Apart from drivers and grooms it also provided employment for blacksmiths, harness makers and feed suppliers. Many of the city's innkeepers and hotel servants depended on the coaches for their livelihood. Goods also had to be transported and the carriers sent their wagons to all parts of the country. The haulage trade was based in South Street where the biggest company, Russell & Co., had its depot in a big warehouse at the Mermaid Inn. Robert Russell's wagons travelled regularly to Falmouth, Southampton, Salisbury and London, a lumbering journey of six days. He also ran a horse-drawn 'van' which reached the capital in thirty-six hours.

These businesses received a severe jolt when the first passenger train, drawn by the steam locomotive *City of Exeter*, arrived at the newly-built St David's station from Bristol on 1 May 1844. A banquet was held to celebrate the event in the flag-bedecked wooden goods shed. Mayor Henry Hooper, the local builder, whose company was responsible for the construction of the station, hosted the celebration, and Isambard Kingdom Brunel, the great engineer who constructed the line, stood on a table to acknowledge the applause of the crowd. Suddenly Exeter was just five hours away from London.

Exeter from Exwick Hill – note the train shed at St David's and the embankment to Queen Street station. Brunel's pump house is beside the bridge on the Exe.

EXETER. *(N.W.)*

Sir Daniel Gooch, the Great Western Railway's locomotive superintendent, rode on the footplate of the first train and reported the journey:

> I worked the train with the Actaeon engine, one of our seven feet class, with six carriages. We left London at 7.30am and arrived at Exeter at 12.30 p.m. having some detention over the hour fixed.
>
> On the return journey we left Exeter at 5.20 p.m. and stopped at the Paddington platform at 10.00 p.m. Sir Thomas Acland, who was with us, went at once to the House of Commons and by 10.30 told the House he had been in Exeter at 5.20.

A consequence of the arrival of the railway was that Exeter had to use London time which required the dean to put the cathedral clock forward by fourteen minutes as Greenwich Mean Time was not generally acknowledged until 1880.

In 1848 Brunel extended the railway line to Teignmouth using a sixty-two arch viaduct to carry the track across St Thomas and over the main roads out of the city. His intention was to use his atmospheric system to power the trains at speeds of up to 68mph. This system pumped air through a pipeline laid between the rails which powered the trains, but unfortunately the project was unsuccessful due to a combination of salty sea air and rats chewing the leather insulation which sealed the driving pipe, and the idea was soon abandoned. A station was built on the viaduct above Cowick Street, which became known as Exeter St Thomas. The new railway line was soon carrying Exonians on excursions to the seaside at Dawlish and Teignmouth.

Exeter's second rail link to London opened in 1860. The London and South Western Railway came into the city via the Blackboy Tunnel at Mount Pleasant and then down the Longbrook Valley which been filled in to allow Exeter's third station to be built below Queen Street. The level of the valley was raised by some 80ft, and the brook piped in. A link was constructed incorporating a tunnel and steep bank down to St David's station. Several branch lines followed to Exmouth, Tiverton and the Teign Valley, while the London and South West mainline continued to Crediton and eventually around the north of Dartmoor to Plymouth.

Exeter continued to be a busy centre for both commerce and transport, while railway excursions brought visitors from far afield. In 1850 the city boasted 148 hotels, inns and taverns, forty of these hostelries were within 200 yards of the city centre. When licensing laws were first introduced in August 1872, which required public houses to close at 11 p.m., several nights of rioting followed.

Produce was still brought in from the country, usually by horse and cart, but also, as the railways expanded, by train. In the mid-nineteenth century fifteen cart loads of fish arrived daily from Topsham until the Exmouth branch line was opened in 1861.

By Victorian times the population of Exeter was approaching 40,000. The Guildhall constables were no longer sufficient to enforce law and order within the city so in 1836 a police force was formed. Hugh Canning was appointed superintendent with a salary of £120 per annum. The new force was divided into day and night-watch police and was made up of the four mace sergeants and six staff bearers, with only the two most junior staff bearers being considered to be full-time police officers. The night watch was commanded by a member of the day force on a rotation basis. The new police force was not free from drunkenness. One officer, John Coles, persuaded a colleague to share a glass with him after which they both found themselves on-board a coach bound for Okehampton where they subsequently became involved in a fight.

By 1885 Exeter had an embryo public transport system. It had begun with horse-drawn buses and in 1881 the Exeter Tramways Co. was given asset to lay and operate lines from London Inn Square through St Sidwell's to the Blackboy turnpike, down Paris Street to Heavitree, as well as to St David's Station. The city council was also considering new technology. In 1870 the Streets Committee discussed the possible purchase of a 12-ton steamroller, at a cost of £425. The roller was actually purchased fifteen years later.

By the late nineteenth century there was still no organised municipal fire brigade. Exeter had become known as the 'fiery city' and the insurance companies, The Sun, West of England, Norwich Union and Royal, employed their own firemen. These relied on natural sources such as ponds, streams and rivers for their water supply and would only attend fires at properties for which the premiums have been fully paid. On one particularly cold night water had to be taken from a frozen pond and a fireman – ironically named Sparkes – fell through the ice and later died.

In 1882 a fire broke out in an oil-store housed in one of the arches on the Quay. It was started by a workman who had foolishly lit a lamp to see his way around the gloomy cavern. Flammable vapours immediately ignited with such force that the ill-fated workman was blown out on to the Quay. Amazingly he was not hurt, but a pair of massive oak doors were flung intact across the river by the force of the blast. The initial explosion also spread blazing oil onto the surface of the river where a schooner and other moored craft were soon ablaze. The flow of the river carried the flames downstream as far as Trew's Weir.

Five years later Exeter was to suffer an even worse conflagration. On Monday 5 September 1887 during a performance of *Romany Rye* at the newly-built Theatre Royal part of the scenery collapsed onto the stage and was ignited by a broken gas mantle. The incident occurred during an interval and though the actors and backstage crew – with the exception of two 'fly men' – all managed to escape nobody bothered to warn the audience. Panic quickly spread amongst the theatregoers when choking smoke began to pour from under the stage curtain into the auditorium. The only escape route was through an inward opening door, which soon became blocked by the crush of people trying to get out. Those trapped were rapidly overcome by smoke. Others managed to reach the roof and many jumped to the street below before ladders could be fetched to rescue them. Firefighters assisted by military and railway crews soon managed to get the fire under control but not before the death toll reached 188.

A contemporary print of the
Theatre Royal fire.

Great bravery was displayed by local resident Mr Edwin Morris of Bedford
Circus, and Able Seaman William Hunt. Hunt was later decorated and promoted
to Leading Seaman, but a soldier named Scattergood died while making a rescue
attempt.

On hearing news of the theatre blaze the Topsham fire brigade turned out to give
assistance. While one of their members went to find a horse the rest of the crew dragged
their fire engine towards Exeter. They were eventually overtaken by the fireman with
the horse which was hastily harnessed to the engine. The firemen climbed aboard but
the weight proved too much for the poor animal and the crew had to run alongside.
Their journey to the burning theatre took them just forty-five minutes.

The Theatre Royal was speedily rebuilt and reopened in 1889. The new
building incorporated a fire curtain and exit doors which opened outwards. As
a result of the Exeter fire these requirements became legal requirements in all
theatres, and also led to the formation of a city fire brigade.

William Pett was appointed as the first Chief Fire Officer of the new Exeter
City Fire Brigade. The fire station was opened in New North Road, just a short
distance from the Theatre Royal, using premises formerly used by the West of
England insurance company fire team. Both the West of England and The Sun
insurance companies donated their fire engines to the new city brigade.

Thanks to Superintendent Pett, Exeter soon lost its 'fiery city' reputation. In
1893 he led a team of Exeter firemen to victory in the Grand International Fire
Tournament in London beating off competition from all parts of the world. The
silver trophy won by the Exeter firemen can still be seen in the Guildhall.

Pett was also a fine cricketer and regularly played for the Exeter Cricket Club.
On one occasion he scored seventy runs in a match against the MCC in which
the redoubtable Dr W.G. Grace was out for a duck.

Guy Fawkes Night on 5 November was celebrated with gusto in Exeter. The celebrations centred on the cathedral yard with a great bonfire outside the West Door of St Peter's. Gangs of youths known as 'Young Exeter' congregated there bringing with them flaming tar barrels, fireworks, and effigies of the pope, bishop and even on one occasion a local businessman and his daughter, which were burnt on the fire. These activities frequently got out of hand and on one occasion the gates of the Close were burnt. In 1867 the mayor, fearing riots, called for military help and the 20th (East Devonshire) Regiment marched into the Close with fixed bayonets. The cathedral authorities, fearing that fire could spread to surrounding buildings, tried to get the tradition stopped but it continued until the end of the century when children's writer, Beatrix Potter, who was clearly unhappy with this tradition noted in 1892 that 'they light bonfires in the Close on 5 November, the rabble are notorious'.

Charles Dickens first visited Exeter to cover the 1835 Election in which Lord John Russell was defeated. Dickens frequented the Turks Head next door to the Guildhall and based some of his characters on the people he saw there. A bar was subsequently named after him. He later bought a house for his parents in Alphington.

Below left: The Guildhall with the Turks Head Inn alongside.

Below right: An ancient passageway into the Cathedral Close.

Other authors also drew inspiration from the city. Anthony Trollope was a frequent visitor as a boy and set his novel *He Knew He Was Right* in Exeter, Bram Stoker's character Jonathan Harker sets off for Transylvania from his office in the Cathedral Close in *Dracula*, while Jane Austen is believed to have used Barton Place at Cowley in *Sense and Sensibility*.

The city witnessed its last public execution in 1868. Seventeen years later Exeter Gaol was the scene of the bizarre attempt to execute John Lee, who became infamous as 'the man they could not hang'. Twenty-year-old Lee was accused of murdering his employer Miss Emma Keyse at her home, the Glen, in Babbacombe where he worked as a servant. He was tried at the Assizes in the Guildhall, rapidly found guilty and sentenced to death. On the morning of his execution, 23 February 1885, he was taken from the condemned cell to the gallows, a temporary affair set up in the shed normally used to house the prison wagon. Lee was placed on the trapdoor with the noose around his neck, but when the hangman, James Berry, pulled the lever the drop failed to work. Lee was taken from the scaffold while alterations to the trapdoor were made. Twice more Berry pulled the level but the gallows again failed to operate. An ashen-faced Lee was returned to his cell and later his sentence commuted to life imprisonment. Berry claimed later that the planks had warped due to overnight rain, but theories persist that Lee had taken the blame for someone of importance and the hangman was bribed. In the 1970s Fairport Convention recorded an album telling the story of John 'Babbacombe' Lee.

The Victorian era saw church building reach its zenith in Exeter with the construction of St Michael and All Angels, Mount Dinham, in 1868 at a cost of £20,000. This magnificent building, with its 220ft spire, was said to be the pinnacle of middle class munificence and faith. Thirty years later it was decided to rebuild St David's church. The new building, which replaced its Georgian predecessor, famous for its 'pepperpot' tower, was consecrated on 9 January 1900, and became the first church in the city to be lit by electricity.

St Michael and All Angels, built in 1868.

The latter part of the nineteenth century saw the rise of a new kind of entrepreneur in Exeter. Henry Frederick Willey was born the son of a cordwainer, or shoemaker, at Sidwell's in 1830. After attending St John's Hospital School Willey was apprenticed to a Mr Vicary, an iron founder who also manufactured gas meters. Willey remained in Vicary's employ until his death in 1868 after which, at the age of forty, he set up his own business. Willey & Co. soon became the largest manufacturing business in Exeter with over 1,000 employees. The firm was at first based in restricted premises on Exe Island but later moved to a new factory near the Basin, where it gave its name to a new thoroughfare, Willeys Avenue. From humble origins H.F. Willey's involvement in local politics saw him appointed first as sheriff and later as mayor.

Another noted Victorian entrepreneur was Harry Hems. Hems, a cutler by trade, made the long journey overland to Florence in order to learn sculpture. He arrived in Exeter in 1868 to work as a stone decorator on the new museum then being built in Queen Street. As he left the station Hems noticed a horseshoe lying in the road and picked it up for luck. Hems set up his own stoneworking business and quickly became very successful supplying the sculptured stonework for the numerous new churches and civic buildings at that time under construction throughout Britain. He built a new workshop, designed by R. Medley Fulford, at the bottom of Longbrook Street. The lucky horseshoe was affixed to the front of the building – which is now a popular restaurant suitably named Harry's – where it remains to this day. During his time at Exeter University pop singer Will Young worked part-time at Harry's.

Despite the growing popularity of railways many Exonians still did not travel far from home. Heavitree, which did not officially become part of Exeter until 1913, remained a popular destination for those who could afford a holiday. Every autumn hundreds flocked to the races held on a point to point course on the outskirts of the village. The journey was made easier when horse-drawn trams were introduced in 1882.

Heavitree did not become part of Exeter until 1913.

One famous visitor to Heavitree was General Charles George Gordon, also known as 'Chinese Gordon' or 'Gordon of Khartoum'. In January 1884 Gordon was staying at the vicarage as guest of the Revd Reginald H. Barnes, who later became Dean of Exeter, when a telegram arrived recalling him to London and then on to the Sudan where he would meet his death at the hands of the Mardi. Gordon's interrupted visit is commemorated by a lamp at the top of Heavitree where the road forks around the Livery Dole Almshouses.

The Revd Barnes was the father of Exeter's two greatest actresses, Irene and Violet Vanbrugh, who were also considered to be the first girls from a 'good family' to tread the boards.

The turn of the century saw Britain engaged in the second Anglo-Boer war in South Africa. This conflict raised Exeter's profile on a national level. As in Elizabethan times when Devon's sea-dogs had fought the Armada, now her soldiers were to the fore in the South African war. General Sir Redvers Buller VC was brought out of retirement to take command, and although he was severely criticised in London for his early defeats his casualty lists were but a mere fraction of the butchers' bills that would follow in Flanders. The tough, hard-riding Buller, whose home was at Downes near Crediton, was much loved by Exonians who in 1905 erected a statue in his honour. It was unveiled in his presence and remains a well-known landmark at the junction of St David's Hill. Other local heroes at a time when the soldiers of the Queen were held in high esteem were Colonel Park who led the charge of the Devonshire regiment at Wagon Hill while attempting to relieve the seize of Ladysmith, and Colonel R.S. Kekewich who found fame as the defender of Kimberley. The Yeomanry, a force of volunteer cavalry, also served in South Africa as did seven members of the Exeter City Fire Brigade.

Kekewich's heroism aided a relative's parliamentary ambitions in the 1906 general election. St George Kekewich of Peamore won the Exeter seat for the

Livery Dole chapel, where Henry VI was welcomed by the civic authorities and where Thomas Benet was burnt at the stake. The lamp was erected in memory of General Gordon.

Above: Chichester Terrace and Southernhay Congregational church, *c.* 1920.

Right: Hoult & Son butcher's shop at No. 154 Sidwell Street, *c.* 1920.

Liberals by 100 votes. It was said that his success came about as many voters mistakenly believed that it was he who had saved Kimberley from the Boers.

The 1910 election was to prove the closest ever fought in Exeter. The first election took place in January when Sir Henry Duke won the seat back for the Conservatives by just twenty-six votes. In a second poll at the end of the year the Liberal candidate, Richard Harold St Maur, defeated Duke by only four votes. The Conservatives called for an enquiry. This was chaired by Mr Justice Ridley and Mr Justice Channell, and looked into claims that some of the Liberal votes were not valid. Ridley was a poor choice as he had been in a similar situation in 1878. Four votes were deemed invalid and in April when the case ended the judges declared that Duke had been elected by 4,777 votes to 4,776. There is a humorous footnote to the affair. As the defeated St Maur bid farewell to his supporters at the railway station, he leaned from the carriage window and declared that they would meet again 'when the city had been cleared of men such as those who had brought charges against him and when the land had been cleared of unjust judges'. A gentleman in the same compartment lowered his newspaper and was seen to be an extremely irate. It was Mr Justice Ridley. As the train pulled out a heated argument ensued.

seven

1900-1939

While Exeter may have entered the twentieth century at the height of Victorian imperial power, a new era of technology was dawning.

The first motorcar, a Benz, was seen in the city in 1897 as part of a circus. A year later a Mr Sturmey passed through Exeter driving his Daimler from John O'Groats to Land's End. Sturmey stayed overnight at the New London Inn where his vehicle attracted considerable attention and inspired engineer Walter Shepherd to build his own car in a workshop on Longbrook Terrace. H.A. Willey tried to encourage Exeter's engineers to launch their own motor industry but the city proved to be too far from Britain's industrial and manufacturing heart in the Midlands.

On 1 January 1904 the registration of motor vehicles became a legal requirement. By that time the city boasted twelve privately owned cars. The registration letters allocated to Exeter were FJ, the initials of the mayor of the

Topsham Road in 1900 and not a car in sight. The buildings in the distance are part of Topsham Barracks.

time, F.J. Widgery. 'FJ 1' was the registration number of a seven horsepower Benz owned by Mr Norman of the brewing company Norman & Pring. Exeter's first woman driver was Miss Katherine Budd who took out her licence on 25 February 1904. At the time anyone could take out a licence and start driving as the test was not introduced until 1935.

Medical technology had also advanced and X-rays had first been used at the Royal Devon and Exeter Hospital in 1898. The Royal prefix was granted by Queen Victoria the following year after the Duke and Duchess of York had visited the hospital and opened the new Victoria wing.

Electric trams were introduced to the city streets in 1905 using tracks laid for the horse trams back in 1881. A new electricity works was built at the city basin to power the trams but the most significant development was the replacement of the three arch Exe Bridge, constructed in 1778, by a single span modern bridge wide enough to carry the tracks. The new bridge was opened on 29 March 1905. The first tram ran just a few days later on 4 April. It was driven by the mayor, Councillor E.C. Parry, who after addressing the crowd from the top deck, descended the stairs, took the control handle and set off from the Guildhall to tour the city. Later in the day the introduction of the tram service was celebrated in the traditional way with a dinner at the New London Inn. This old coaching inn was soon to adapt to the changing times by converting its stables into a garage for fifty cars.

The trams quickly became a major success. Twelve tramcars ran over various routes across the city. A few years earlier a census had shown that more than 10,000 people crossed Exe Bridge for the city centre every Saturday night so it was not surprising that the trams proved such a popular form of transport. On Sundays the motormen (as the drivers were known) were instructed to drive past churches as quietly as possible so not to disturb the services. The trams were generally safe but in July 1907 a tramcar collided with a lorry on St David's Hill. The lorry overturned and the motorman lost control. As a result the tram

The 1905 Exe Bridge.

Opposite above: The first tram, driven by Mayor E.C. Perry, outside the Guildhall 1905.

Opposite below: The tram depot.

careered down the hill, jumped the track on the curve at the bottom, and hit the station building, fortunately without injuring anyone.

The railways also continued to be well used. Here too technology was improving all the time. On 9 May 1904 the Great Western locomotive *City of Truro* passed through Exeter St David's Station hauling the 'Ocean Mails' special from Plymouth and on the run down Wellington Bank in Somerset became the first steam locomotive to exceed 100mph. Exonians made full use of the railways for weekend excursions to the seaside at Exmouth, Dawlish and Teignmouth.

Not long afterwards Exeter saw aeroplanes for the first time. In 1911 the city was a staging post in the 'Circuit of Britain' air race with competitors landing at what would become the Whipton showground, later the home of the Devon County Show. Among the competitors was American aviator S.F. Cody. Cody later became an advisor to the British Army before being killed in a flying accident. Earlier in his life he had appeared in a Wild West show and was frequently mistaken for his namesake Buffalo Bill Cody as he habitually wore buckskins and grew his hair long. The actual Buffalo Bill – William Fredrick Cody – came to Exeter in 1903 with his world famous western show. The show was part of countrywide tour and was brought to town on three massive trains. The cast included Japanese and Mexican roughriders, Cossacks, Bedouins, and South American gauchos. The grand finale was a re-enactment of Custer's Last Stand and an attack by Red Indians on the Deadwood Stage. Over 500 horses were used in the show which even included a herd of bison and Texas longhorn cattle.

A growing form of entertainment was the cinema. The first moving picture shows had been seen at the travelling funfair. The Victoria Hall in Queen Street, a scaled-down version of London's Albert Hall, showed films in summer but reverted to holding dances in the winter. The Hippodrome, partly financed by the music hall impresario Fred Karno, also showed films in 1908, but the first real cinema was the Empire Electric in high Street which opened in 1911. It was followed by the King's Hall, in Okehampton Street, now a Christian Fellowship church, the Palladium in Paris Street, and the Hippodrome, later burnt down in the Blitz and now the site of Boots in the High Street.

Fore Street, Exeter,

Fore Street – looking towards the city centre.

Fred Karno was born in Waterbeer Street in 1866 and was responsible for both Charlie Chaplin and Stan Laurel's early breaks into showbusiness. His slapstick style of comedy was extremely popular and during the First World War British soldiers referred themselves as 'Fred Karno's Army' in a marching song sung to the tune of 'The Church is One Foundation' written by Exeter man Samuel Sebastian Wesley, the one time cathedral organist. Another well-known comedian to grow up in Exeter was Tommy Cooper, who lived with his parents in Fords Road, St Thomas and attended Mount Radford school in the thirties.

Sport was becoming popular at this time and Exonians eagerly supported their local teams. They flocked to the County Ground in St Thomas where the Exeter Football (Rugby) club played their matches. The stadium was built in 1890 and originally included a steeply banked cycle track around the pitch. Six thousand people attended the first ever match played by the New Zealand All Blacks in the UK. This took place on 16 September 1905 with the All Blacks beating Devon 55-4. Photographs of the event show the New Zealand players wearing Panama hats to keep off the sun!

Up at the other end of the town Exeter City Football Club turned professional in 1904. The team played on a site in St James Road and became known as the Grecians. This had been the name given to the local boys of St Sidwell's while their rivals inside the city walls went by the name of Trojans. Ten years later the club toured Brazil and played against the national side. On the voyage home the team's ship almost became the first victim of the First World War as a warning shot was fired at it by a patrolling Royal Navy warship.

Despite the rapid growth of technology Exeter had areas where people lived in great poverty. In the West Quarter many lived from hand to mouth and children were glad of the farthing breakfast, a mug of cocoa and a large slice of bread spread with margarine and jam, subsidised by charity. This part of Exeter remained a tough place where the police still patrolled in pairs but the city remained relatively free of serious crime.

St Thomas Rowing Club –
West of England Champions,
1907/08.

More affluent Exonians would shortly be able to enjoy the delights of Deller's Café which opened on 5 December 1916 when its first customers were soldiers. This lavish and extremely popular meeting place was built above Lloyds Bank which replaced the Half Moon Hotel on the corner of Bedford Street in 1912. Deller's boasted a two-tier dining room surrounded by balconies, the first level of which was surrounded by alcoves which could be discreetly closed off with a curtain for private meetings and assignations. The café became the venue for tea dances, parties, formal dinners, a meeting place for theatre-goers, even whist drives. It was the scene for many engagements and remains one of Exeter's best-loved buildings of the twentieth century.

During the First World War Exeter was a long way from the front, but the conflict still took its toll on the population. Many Exonians volunteered to join the Devonshire Regiment, nicknamed the Bloody Eleventh, and doubtless some of them were with the 2nd Devons in France when the final German offensive was delayed at Bois Des Buttes on 27 May 1918. In a last stand action the Devons held out against tanks, aircraft and an unremitting artillery barrage, giving the rest of the army vital time to regroup. The commanding officer, Col. Anderson-Morshead, was killed and twenty-three officers and 528 men were either killed, wounded or taken prisoner. The Devonshire Regiment was later awarded the Croix de Guerre by the French government for their bravery. The 128 (Wessex) Field Ambulance, Royal Army Medical Corps of the Territorial Army, were also commended for their gallantry and awarded this honour after evacuating 2,000 civilians under artillery fire at St Amand in France between 22-25 October 1918.

King George V visited wounded soldiers at Exeter in 1915. Several military hospitals had been set up in the city and the King became the first reigning monarch to be driven through the city streets in a motor car. After arriving at St David's Station he and Queen Mary toured the Eye Infirmary, then known as No. 1 (Military) Hospital, and also visited No. 5 Hospital at the castle.

Below left: The interior of Deller's Café.

Below right: The entrance to Northernhay Gardens with the City War Memorial in the background.

Two notable local happenings occurred in 1917. A severe winter saw the Exe freeze over allowing Exonians to walk across and skate on the river. The thaw that followed caused severe flooding. Wartime shortages of manpower led to neglect of the tram system and that year an accident occurred on 17 March when tramcar No. 12 ran out of control down Fore Street hill, collided with a horse and cart, pushing the vehicle through a shop window which killed the horse, and then crashed on Exe Bridge. The tram driver remained at his controls and was injured along with three passengers. Tragically a woman passenger, Mrs Mary Findlay, was killed in the accident. The conductress managed to jump clear but suffered cuts and shock.

The war had taken a terrible toll and to commemorate Exeter's war dead an impressive memorial was built in Northernhay Gardens. It was designed by John Angel, who was born in Newton Abbot but grew up in Exeter and it was unveiled on 24 July 1923 by Admiral David Beatty who had commanded the British fleet at the Battle of Jutland in 1916. Meanwhile the prominent architect Sir Edwin Lutyens was commissioned to design the County War Memorial

Flooding at the Quay in 1917.

An accident in Fore Street, 1906.

which was built on the cathedral green. This was dedicated in 1921, and was attended by the then Prince of Wales, later briefly King Edward VIII. The Prince would later return in 1927 to open the northern bypass through the Hoopern Valley and as president of the recently created University of the South West, he laid the foundation stone for the Washington Singer building on the intended campus site. The new university had developed from the Exeter College of Science and Art at the Albert Memorial Museum and was at that time housed in Gandy Street using premises which are now the Phoenix Arts Centre.

The 1920s saw great efforts made to clear Exeter of its slums. The city's first council houses, 'forty-two workmen's dwellings' had been built in Isca Road, St Thomas, in 1907 with rents inclusive of rates set at five shillings (25p) per week. In 1927 new estates were built at Burnthouse Lane and Buddle Lane to re-house the families from the West Quarter and other poor parts of the city. Burnthouse Lane was then considered so far from the city that its new inhabitants referred to it as 'Siberia'. Many of the men living on the new estate worked at Willey's foundry and rode to work on bicycles. To make life easier for their employees the company built the suspension bridge at Trews Weir in 1935 allegedly to enable the men to 'go home for dinner'.

Efforts to improve the health of Exeter's children had resulted in the building of the Crippled Children's Hospital at Buckerell Bore. The hospital was opened by the Duke and Duchess of York – later King George VI and Queen Elizabeth – in 1927 and a cot was named after their baby daughter, the newly born Princess Elizabeth. Later the name would be changed to the Princess Elizabeth Orthopaedic Hospital. A driving force behind the building of the hospital was local philanthropist Lady Georgiana Buller, daughter of the venerated General Buller. In 1930 the era of the Poor Law ended and the Heavitree Road Workhouse became redundant. The infirmary was taken over by the council and became the City Hospital specialising in maternity services and care of the elderly. Lady Buller also played a major role is establishing the St Loye's Foundation in 1937 which set up a rehabilitation college for the disabled.

The University of the South West (1922). The main building was in Gandy Street, behind the museum. It is now the Phoenix Arts Centre.

The West Quarter and Quay
from the air.

Increased motor traffic saw the city install its first set of traffic lights at the junction of Queen Street and High Street early in 1929. The High Street was still the main thoroughfare for traffic travelling from London to Cornwall. Later in the year the *Express and Echo* reported that the new system was respected by the majority of motorists but difficulties still occurred when country folk came to market on Fridays.

That summer locally-born entrepreneur Leonard Glanfield introduced dirt track racing – later known as speedway – to Exeter. It was an immediate success and regularly attracted crowds of 10,000 and more to the County Ground. The autocratic Glanfield brought down international stars from the London tracks on a regular basis but the attraction gradually faded and the speedway track closed midway through 1931. Greyhound racing was also introduced. The first meetings were held at Oak Marsh, Alphington, where the 'hare' was propelled by means of a rope attached to the back axle of an old car. In 1931 the sport moved to the County Ground where it remained until the late 1990s.

The 1930s saw many major improvements to Exeter. The outer bypass was opened in 1936 to take through traffic away from the city centre, but many drivers still preferred to travel through the town. The new road ran from Countess Wear to Pinhoe Road, crossing the Honiton Road by means of a flyover. Alongside the roundabout at Middlemoor the new headquarters for the Devon Constabulary was built.

Boots corner. The junction of Queen Street and High Street was the first location in Exeter to have electric traffic lights.

St Lawrence church in High Street – destroyed in 1942.

Sidwell Street – the tram pole wires are clearly visible.

1931 saw the end of trams in Exeter. The slow speed trams were causing congestion in the narrow city streets and as a result the council decided to replace them with 'motor buses'. The buses had already replaced trams on the Alphington route, and on 19 August 1931 car No.14 toured all the remaining lines before stopping at the Guildhall, where Mr E.C. Perry, who as mayor had driven the first tram, took the controls for the final journey to the depot at the bottom of Paris Street. The tram was followed by a bus, which continued on its way to Heavitree. At the depot the tram turned in, stopped, and the power was switched off for the final time. Exeter's short but popular tram era was over. Four cars had already been sold to Halifax in Yorkshire while the others were taken to Plymouth. The control handle of the last tram was silver plated, and is kept among the city's treasures in the Guildhall.

Around this time the original fire station in New North Road was deemed too small to house the brigade's modern appliances. A site was selected at Danes Castle and the new station was built at a cost of £16,640. It opened on 25 July 1932.

Exeter may have become a comfortable county town but the hangman still paid regular visits to the County Gaol. Between 1900 and 1943 eleven men and one woman took the short walk from the condemned cell to the gallows, which had been re-housed in a shed alongside the main cell block. The most notorious

High Street in the 1930s. An early double-decker bus is in evidence.

murderer of this time was Mrs Bryant, who poisoned her husband with arsenic and was hanged by Tom Pierrepoint, assisted by his nephew Albert, at Exeter on 15 July 1936. It is said that Mrs Bryant's black hair turned white during her time in the condemned cell. 'Uncle' Tom returned to Exeter to carry out the prison's last execution, that of Gordon Trenoweth on 6 April 1943. Trenoweth had battered to death sixty-one-year-old Albert Bateman at Falmouth.

During the thirties Exeter gained three cinemas. The Gaumont in North Street opened for the first time on Whit Monday 1932 with a showing of *Sunshine Susie*. The Savoy (later the ABC) followed in 1936 and was built on the site of the famous London Inn which had been demolished in 1930. Finally, and perhaps most impressive of all, was the Odeon which opened on 30 August 1937 with *The Charge of the Light Brigade* starring Errol Flynn and David Niven. The name Odeon, although of Greek origin was also an acronym of 'Otto Deutsch Entertains Our Nation', Deutsch being the owner of the cinema chain. The new cinema could seat a total of 1,920 moviegoers, 1,176 in the stalls and a further 744 in the circle. A restaurant was also included. Not surprisingly these magnificent new picture houses soon put the old fleapits out of business.

Regular air travel became part of Exeter life in 1937. An early aerodrome had been sited in Heavitree near the gallows early in the century but when the city council decided to establish an airport they chose build it on ninety acres of land at Waterslade Farm close to Clyst Honiton, a site chosen by Commander William Forbes-Sempill following an aerial survey. Exeter's new airport was still a grass field when flying began on 31 May 1937 and the terminal was a tent, but the local flying club soon established a bar at the rear of a hangar. Two airlines operated from Exeter both using ten-seater De Havilland Dragon Rapide biplanes. The airport was managed by an American, Whitney Straight, the son of Mrs L.K. Elmhirst of Dartington Hall, who had been the youngest pilot in England having gained his licence at the age of sixteen. Straight was also a top racing driver having won the 1934 Donington Grand Prix and then the 1935 South African race in a Maserati. He would become a distinguished fighter pilot with several 'kills' before being himself shot down. He was captured but escaped and managed to return to England, ending the war as a highly-decorated group captain. Whitney Straight later became managing director of BOAC, later British Airways, and also a director of Rolls Royce.

Exeter Airport, its new terminal building recently completed, was officially opened by Sir Kingsley Wood, Secretary of State for Air on 30 July 1938. The opening ceremony attracted a crowd of 30,000 who were entertained by a flying display courtesy of three crack German aerobatic pilots. One of the pilots, Emil Kropf, acknowledged the crowd's applause with a Nazi salute.

1939 saw the opening of the new city swimming baths in Heavitree Road. Up until then bathers either swam in the Exe above Head Weir or used the indoors baths in King Street, now the car park below the central library. At the outdoor pool changing huts stood on the bank, below the railway viaduct in Bonhay Road. The bathing area was overseen by Archie Matthews, the one-legged swimming instructor. Swimmers occasionally found themselves accompanied

Filmgoers queue to see Johnny Weissmuller in *Tarzan the Apeman* at the Gaumont.

by a dead sheep or dog floating downstream and also had to avoid nesting swans. Bonhay Road also bade farewell to its cattle market in 1939, and the herds of cattle and sheep that were driven to it on the hoof every week. The new cattle market was opened at the corner of Alphington Road and Marsh Barton.

Exeter in the 1930s was a comfortable, quiet county town but the clouds of war were gathering and everything was about to change.

eight

The Second World War

When the Second World War broke out on Sunday 3 September 1939 Exeter was not unprepared. Since the Munich Crisis twelve months previously precautions had been put into place. Air-raid shelters had been built, emergency water tanks set up, and gas masks issued. Soon the iron railings around the cathedral green and the gardens in Southernhay would disappear to help the war effort while evacuated children from London and other large cities began to arrive and were lodged with local families. Two well-known characters who were evacuated to Exeter as children were Rabbi Lionel Blue and Danny La Rue. Gardens and spare ground were soon turned into vegetable patches and allotments as the country was urged to 'Dig for Victory'. When the Royal Devon and Exeter Hospital appealed for surplus produce to feed the patients the village of Copplestone alone supplied three tons of potatoes.

The blackout was imposed and headlamps on motor vehicles were restricted. This led to many accidents including one in Burnthouse Lane where a bus collided with a newly built air-raid shelter causing several casualties.

Wartime firemen on an exercise at the Quay.

An early realisation of the conflict came in December when the city's adopted ship, the cruiser HMS *Exeter*, along with the *Ajax* and the *Achilles*, fought a fierce action with the German pocket battleship *Graf Spree* in the South Atlantic. The action, known as the Battle of the River Plate, saw the *Exeter* badly damaged with many casualties, but the *Graf Spree*, also seriously weakened, was eventually forced to seek shelter in Montevideo harbour, where she scuttled herself. When the battle-scarred HMS *Exeter* eventually returned to her home port, members of her crew were brought to Exeter where they marched through the streets to the Guildhall. In 1942 the ship was sunk during the Battle of the Java Sea by Japanese aircraft. Her battle ensign hangs in the cathedral where a stained-glass window is dedicated to those who lost their lives onboard the ship. Part of the *Exeter*'s original mast was preserved beside the canal at Double Locks, having once been used as balance beams on the lock gates. In the summer of 2004 the current HMS *Exeter* passed over the spot where her predecessor was sunk, and a wreath was thrown into the sea.

On 14 May 1940 Anthony Eden made a radio appeal for men between forty and sixty-five years of age to establish the Land Defence Volunteers, later to become known as the Home Guard. The 1st Devonshire (Loyal City of Exeter) Battalion was formed and served throughout the war. 2,000 volunteers, many of whom were ex-soldiers, answered the initial appeal. The Home Guard established their headquarters in St Pancras Lane and training sessions were held in the Higher Market. Other units were also formed including a light anti-aircraft battery, made up of Southern Railway employees, to defend the railway depot at Exmouth Junction.

The recently-opened airport became RAF Station Exeter in July 1940 and within weeks its fighter squadrons were engaged in the Battle of Britain. 213 and 87 Squadrons, equipped with Hawker Hurricane aircraft, were the first to see action when they intercepted 165 enemy bombers heading for Portland. Two twin-engined Junkers 88s were shot down before the German fighters arrived, and in the ensuing dogfight the Exeter-based Hurricanes destroyed three Messerschmitt BF109Es and damaged two ME110s with the loss of four of their own aircraft. 610 Squadron relieved the 213 in September as the Battle of Britain came to a close. On 12 December one of the 610 pilots shot down a Heinkel bomber. He was Flight Lieutenant Whitney Straight, the former Exeter airport operator.

Exeter suffered its first aerial attack on the night of 16 August 1940 when a single aircraft dropped five bombs on the outskirts of St Thomas. It was the first time Exeter had heard a shot fired in anger since the Civil War 300 years before. A month later the city suffered its first casualties when four brothers were killed when a bomb destroyed their home in Blackboy Road. The death toll could well have been greater as at the time the bomb exploded – 10.20 p.m. – a double-decker bus, crammed with cinemagoers returning from the Gaumont, was approaching. Fortunately the blast was deflected and none of the passengers were hurt. Altogether, Exeter would be the target of seventeen raids as a result of being on the Luftwaffe flight path to Bristol, Birmingham and other major cities. In total the air-raid sirens sounded 366 times.

In the spring of 1941 the airfield was attacked five times. A low level raid by three bombers damaged sixteen aircraft and wrecked the main hanger on 5 April. This was followed by a heavy night raid on 12/13 May. The officers' and sergeants' messes were both destroyed and much of the station was set on fire, including a defiant night fighter of (307) Polish squadron. The Poles had only arrived two weeks before the attack, but one crew reacted quickly. Sector control at Poltimore House were caught unawares but, acting on their own initiative, two sergeants got their aircraft airborne and managed to shoot down one of the attacking Heinkel 111 bombers. On their return the crew were reprimanded for their lack of discipline, while the 'erk' (RAF mechanic) who started the engine and guided the Defiant onto the runway was awarded the Polish Cross of Valour.

The series of major attacks known as the Exeter Blitz took place in late April and May 1942 and followed an RAF raid on the north German town of Lübeck. Lübeck was, like Exeter, not considered to be a significant military target but its ancient wooden buildings burnt rapidly as the result of area bombing. The raid is said to have incensed Hitler to the extent that he called for the Baedeker guidebook and demanded that Britain's most beautiful cities – Bath, Canterbury, Norwich, as well as Exeter – be destroyed.

Exeter was the first to be attacked on 23 April when forty-five aircraft, comprising of Donnier 217's, Junkers 88s and Heinkel 111s, arrived over the city but found the target was covered by low cloud. A stick of four bombs fell on Okehampton Street, in close proximity to the main railway line. Five people were killed. One enemy plane, a Donnier Do217e was shot down over Axminster by an RAF Beaufighter. The crew baled out and were taken prisoner.

The following night the raiders returned and this time succeeded in bombing their target which had been illuminated by candle flares. Serious damage was caused to Paris Street, King Street, Pennsylvania and Wonford while bombs also fell in many other locations. Altogether seventy-three people were killed including four at the Abbot's Lodging in the Cathedral Close.

The main raid came on Sunday 4 May. By now many Exonians were making the nightly trek out of Exeter to seek shelter in the surrounding countryside. Nevertheless the majority of the people were still in their homes or air-raid shelters when the raiders arrived at 1.36 a.m. Forty aircraft, mainly twin engine Junkers 88s, flew up the Exe estuary aided by a full moon, and delivered 160 high explosive bombs and 10,000 incendiaries, a total payload of seventy-five tonnes. Vast swathes of the city centre totalling more than thirty acres were destroyed, including much of High Street and Sidwell Street, while Paris Street, the residential area of Newtown and South Street, including the Lower Market also suffered extensive damage. Fires burned all around the cathedral, which miraculously was only hit by a single bomb. That bomb destroyed the Chapel of St John in the south quire aisle and also seriously damaged the organ. The tail fin of the bomb was salvaged and can still be seen in the cathedral education department. At the outbreak of war the cathedral authorities had sensibly removed most of the ancient treasures, including the medieval bishop's throne, and stained glass to a place of safety. The Guildhall, the front of which was

Bomb damage in
Pennsylvania.

Bedford Street. This replaced
Bedford Circus, bombed in
1942, and has now been
demolished.

Deller's Café – a corner of the
first floor.

protected a by a brick wall, also miraculously escaped damage but many of the city's other landmarks were hit. The beautiful Georgian Bedford Circus was gutted by fire and later the decision was taken to demolish the shell for safety reasons. A similar fate befell the burnt out façade of the Commercial Union building in High Street and the much-loved Deller's Café.

The City Hospital in Heavitree Road received several direct hits. Eighteen patients were killed and important medical records destroyed. One of the nurses, Mrs Emily Knee, was awarded the George Medal, the highest civilian decoration, for her efforts in saving patients. Air-Raid Warden Ernest Howard and War Reserve Constable V. Hutchings were similarly decorated.

The fire brigade, reinforced by units from as far afield as Plymouth, Bristol and Bournemouth, battled to quench the flames and control the fires which spread along the length of High Street and Sidwell Street. Water was pumped from the river at the Quay and thousands of feet of canvas hosepipe snaked through the streets. Other fire fighters, men and women, bravely took supplies of petrol through the blazing city to refuel the pumps. 223 people died in the four raids of the Exeter Blitz. Ninety-five people were seriously injured while those slightly injured numbered 488.

Several churches were destroyed including St Sidwell's, St Lawrence, St James, Southernhay Congregational, St Stephen's, and the Bedford chapel, while St Mary Arches lost its roof to fire. The Cathedral Choristers School and St John's Hospital School were both destroyed while St Luke's Diocesan College and the City Library suffered serious damage, including the loss of an estimated one million books, while twenty-six hotels and public houses were destroyed. Among them were the Globe Hotel in Cathedral Yard which at first seemed to have survived only to burn down hours later, the Chevalier Inn on Fore Street, the Seven Stars Hotel in Okehampton Street, which was already partly demolished, and both the Old Golden Lion in Market Street and the New Golden Lion in Guinea Street.

Two residents inspect a bomb crater alongside Union Road.

During the Exeter Blitz the Polish night-fighter pilots of 307 Squadron shot down three Junkers 88s and damaged another. One of these aircraft crashed onto the football pitch at Topsham Barracks.

Within forty-eight hours of the Luftwaffe's departure Exeter received a royal visit. King George VI and Queen Elizabeth visited the city to offer sympathy and support and toured areas where royalty had never been seen before. They stopped twice, at Okehampton Road opposite Emmanuel church, and The Triangle at the bottom of the badly hit Paris Street, to view the damage. At both locations people crowded around to welcome the royals, who also visited the Guildhall and the cathedral. Inside the latter they were shown the damage to the quire where the King picked up a piece of shrapnel and commented that it should be turned into armaments and returned to whence it came.

Altogether Exeter suffered seventeen air raids between August 1940 and December 1942. The railway was frequently targeted, especially the engine sheds at Exmouth Junction, and three months later bombs also fell on the main line 600 yards from St David's station. Damage to track and embankment was soon repaired while in the meantime passengers were ferried by other means of transport between St David and St Thomas stations. During another raid eight men were killed when an air-raid shelter at the Red Cow level crossing suffered a direct hit. There was also a grim incident when a parachute mine landed in Exwick cemetery uprooting a large tree and scattering tombstones, coffins and bones over a large area.

The last air raid on Exeter took place during the morning of 30 December 1942 when a flight of Focke Wulf 190 fighter bombers made a daylight hit and run attack hitting Hollaway Street, where four houses and a block of flats were completely destroyed, and Isca Road, killing eighteen people and injuring 100 others. One of the enemy aircraft was shot down and crashed in a field off Barley Lane.

An unexploded bomb is removed from Culverdale Road.

By 1943 American GIs were arriving in Exeter as part of the build-up to the invasion of Europe. American soldiers, including the 382 Medical Company US Army, were based at Topsham Barracks. Many more were stationed in temporary facilities previously used by the British Army at the County Ground stadium in St Thomas. It was here that world heavyweight boxing champion Joe Louis made a morale boosting visit and is reputed to have fought a demonstration bout. For the first and only time in its history Exeter saw racial segregation, with the river as the dividing line. White GIs were generally based within the city while the black soldiers were billeted in St Thomas and not allowed to cross the river into the town. During this time the *Express and Echo* reported that following a night-time brawl on the main up line platform at St David's station a young black sailor was stabbed to death. Thanks to the blackout nobody saw clearly what happened but awaiting passengers reported seeing a fight between sailors and soldiers. The body of the victim was found on the footbridge leading from the platform to the exit. The Military Police interrogated several people and carried out an unsuccessful search for the murder weapon.

The 29th United States Naval Construction Battalion arrived in Exeter from Ireland in September 1943 to build a major supply depot at Seabrook on the Topsham Road. The depot was built in three months and housed 2,000 Seabees who were assembling supplies for D-Day. Railway sidings connected the depot with the Exmouth to Exeter branch line and a dock was constructed on the nearby canal to enable ships to be loaded and unloaded. At the end of the war

Damaged property in Union Road.

the depot was handed over to the Royal Navy and it continued to operate until the late 1990s. Local folklore claims that, like so many military sites, a huge amount of equipment including trucks, jeeps and a large number of Harley Davidson motorcycles were buried on the site.

In the spring of 1944 the marshland beside the Exe estuary had become a vast military camp as the troops were assembled for the long-awaited invasion of Europe. Shortly before D-Day these troops were joined briefly by a detachment of the Oxford and Buckingham Light Infantry who were preparing for a vital task. Consequently Bridge Road at Countess Wear was closed for several nights to allow these men to practice an important glider borne attack. The bridges over the river and the canal closely resembled those that crossed the River Orne and Caen canal in Normandy. At 11.00 p.m. on 5 June three gliders landed in France close to what has become known as 'Pegasus Bridge' and successfully prevented enemy reinforcements from crossing and reaching the allied bridgehead.

At Honiton Clyst the RAF had suddenly been replaced at the airport by the USAAF. It now became known as Station 463 and on 14 April became home to four squadrons of the 440th Troop Carrying Group. The 440th was equipped with forty-five C47 Dakota aircraft and CG-4A Hadrian gliders. There followed an intensive spell of glider-towing practice before the unit carried airborne troops and paratroopers to France on D-Day. Once this vital mission had been completed and landing fields established in Normandy the Dakotas became flying ambulances and began ferrying the wounded back to England as well as carrying supplies to the front line.

Other preparations for D-Day had been under construction at Willey's factory for several months. These were sections of the massive Mulberry artificial harbour which was eventually floated across the Channel to enable the allies to unload vital supply ships as rapidly as possible. The work at Willey's had continued despite the loss of the factory roof in an air raid. Construction was maintained under the protection of 500 tarpaulin sheets.

After D-Day the war rather left Exeter behind and even the Home Guard was stood down on 31 December 1944. Victory in Europe was celebrated with an outdoor service at the cathedral, and dancing in the streets, while a charity speedway meeting was staged in Exwick Fields. When the fighting finally ended with the dropping of the atom bomb on Japan in August 1945 the people of Exeter turned to the task of rebuilding their city.

nine

Modern Times

With the majority of the city centre destroyed, redevelopment was the major concern in 1945. To help the city council rebuild, a professional town planner was engaged. Thomas Sharp was one of several architects and planners already engaged in post-war redevelopment. He spent several weeks in Exeter surveying the damage, considering the needs of the business community, and studying the movement of population into and out of the city. His ideas were published in a book entitled *Exeter Phoenix* in 1946.

Sharp's plans were displayed in the burnt-out shell of the city library, and the centrepiece of the exhibition was a scale model of the city centre. His exciting proposals for the rebuilding of Exeter included an inner bypass, which circled the city walls. The plan included a cloverleaf junction at Shilhay, and a dual carriageway along Exe Street and through a tunnel under Northernhay before joining New North Road at a roundabout. Roundabouts were also planned for the junctions of High Street with North and South Streets, and at Eastgate. Sharp planned to recapture some of Exeter's medieval glory by having the top storeys

J. Lethbridge, poulterer and game dealer, at No.183 Cowick Street. The author's grandfather, Joe Lethbridge, stands in the centre of his workforce. The young boy is Dick Lethbridge, who later took over the business with his brother Ted.

of the shops overlapping the street. He also suggested that Cowick Street be bypassed and become a pedestrian zone.

Sadly the council were not prepared to meet what they considered to be the excessive cost of the land required for Sharp's vision. Not all his ideas were dismissed however and his recommendation for an industrial estate at Marsh Barton became a reality, and must have far exceeded his original expectations. Sharp also recommended that a pedestrian shopping street should be built to the south of High Street. This was adopted and would launch the redevelopment. Princess Elizabeth laid the foundation stone during a visit to Exeter on 21 October 1949 after which the area became known as Princesshay. Two years later King George VI and Queen Elizabeth, accompanied by Princess Margaret, attended a service at the cathedral to celebrate the completion of the restoration work.

Work to clear rubble from the bomb-sites had already begun This was dumped in the valley of the Shute Brook below Southernhay and would provide the foundations for a new inner bypass, Western Way, the first section of which ran from Paris Street to Bull Meadow wall and was in use by 1955.

The rebuilding of High Street continued through the fifties and sixties. Colsons (now Dingles), which dated back to 1792, and had been severely damaged in 1942, was rebuilt while continuing to trade. Its top floor restaurant became popular with shoppers as the place to take afternoon tea while fashion models paraded between the tables displaying the latest styles. The refurbished store also boasted Exeter's first escalators. Another major impact on the High Street was the opening of the new Marks and Spencer store, complete with a cafeteria, on the corner of Castle Street.

Paris Street would be completely redeveloped and eventually, in the sixties, became home to the new bus station and civic centre. Bobbys (now Debenhams) department store moved from Fore Street to a new tower block on London Inn Square.

Princesshay. The starting point for Exeter's post-war redevelopment has now been demolished to make way for a new shopping complex.

High Street, viewed from
the top of Debenhams. The
cathedral can just be seen
above the rebuilt High Street.

The rebuilding of Sidwell Street took longer. During the fifties temporary shops lined the road above the bombed church. On the bomb-site across the street a preserved whale was displayed for a short time by travelling showmen. Apparently the whale toured the country on the back of a lorry and by the time it stopped touring was more preservative than whale.

At the other end of town the bomb damaged Lower Market was demolished, South Street widened and new shops and buildings sprang up across this decimated area. British Home Stores opened a store at the lower end of High Street. On the other side of the road the new Chevalier Tavern opened in 1956 next to the indoor Pannier Market above which was built St George's Hall, which in its early days also housed the corn exchange.

Development continued into the seventies with Broadwalk House, an office complex, being built along the city wall at the top of Southernhay and later the Southgate Hotel replaced Trinity Yard and a row of Georgian properties.

1959 saw the Exe Bridge end of Cowick Street partly demolished, the remainder, along with much of Alphington Street, was pulled down a few years later to make way for a complex new road system, which would eventually feed onto the two new bridges. Exe Bridge North was opened to traffic in 1969 and was followed by its southern twin in 1972. When both bridges were complete the 1905 single span bridge was demolished.

One reason why this much-loved Exe Bridge was removed was the great flood of 1960, when the bridge had caused a bottleneck as the surging floodwater tried to funnel under it. Twice during that exceptionally wet autumn the Exe broke its banks and swept through the old flood plain to a depth of up to 6ft. The flood water reached the Crawford Inn in Alphington Road and the St Thomas Methodist church at the far end of Cowick Street. 2,500 houses were flooded and Exwick and Alphington also suffered badly.

The first flood struck at midday on Thursday 27 October with a reported 42,000 tons of water per minute sweeping through St Thomas. Workers

The junction of Alphington Street and Cowick Street, c. 1968. The Cowick Street properties are in the process of being demolished.

The floods in Cowick Street, 1960.

returning to their homes west of the Exe were taken through the flooded streets on lorries or DUKW amphibious vehicles brought in by the army. A second flood followed a month later. Consequently many properties, particularly in Okehampton Street, were so badly damaged that they had to be demolished.

Over the next twenty years a flood prevention scheme was created covering the area from Exwick Fields to Head Weir. The 1905 bridge was replaced by the two modern crossings, which allowed a much greater flow of water to pass under them in times of flooding. Attractive terraced riverside walks were created from Head Weir to the Quay. These have become popular with cyclists, skaters, dog walkers and those just out for a gentle stroll along the river bank. The value

of the scheme was seen in the autumn of 2000 when in conditions similar to those of forty years before the flood water was kept under control despite, on one occasion, coming within inches of the top of the protective banks.

Traffic crossing Exe Bridge in the late 1960s. The surrounding buildings have since been demolished.

In 1955 the University of the South West received its charter and became the University of Exeter. The following year the Queen visited the campus accompanied by the Duke of Edinburgh to confer the rolls. Two of the university's best-known graduates have been children's writer J.K. Rowling of *Harry Potter* fame and pop singer Will Young. 1956 also saw Exeter establish a twinning agreement with Rennes, the capital of Brittany. Since then Exeter has also twinned with Bad Homburg in Germany (1965), Terracina in Italy (1986) and Yaroslavl in Russia.

The cinema and radio remained the major sources of entertainment during the fifties despite the increasing popularity of television. The sale of television sets was boosted by the decision to broadcast live coverage of the coronation in June 1953. The author well remembers seeing a group of people huddled on deckchairs in the rain on the pavement outside a 'prefab' in Sidwell Street watching the coronation on a newfangled television in the shop window.

Variety shows were also popular and many of the stars of the day including Tony Hancock, Max Bygraves, the Billy Cotton Bandshow, singers Alma Coogan and Dickie Valentine, and even radio ventriloquist Peter Brough and his dummy Archie Andrews attracted full houses to the Savoy. Later, in the sixties, variety gave way to pop. Cliff Richard and the Shadows, the Beatles, the Rolling Stones, Manfred Mann, Jerry and the Pacemakers, and many other top groups and singers appeared in the city. The Beatles probably attracted the most attention; The 'fab four' first appeared at the Savoy as second feature to Chris Montez but returned to top the bill during the height of Beatlemania in the autumn of 1963.

Sadly this era also saw the end of the Theatre Royal. After seventy consecutive Christmas pantomimes, which drew theatregoers from all parts of the county, the theatre closed in the autumn of 1962 and was demolished the following year. The Royal was replaced by the Northcott Theatre which opened on the university campus in 1967. Although the Northcott has staged many fine productions, in which many future stars have appeared, it has never really been regarded by Exonians with the same affection as the Theatre Royal. In recent summers the Northcott Company has traditionally staged an open air Shakespeare play in Northernhay Gardens under the shadow of Rougemont Castle.

In the fifties the Christmas trading season was of much shorter duration. It was heralded in Exeter by the arrival of Father Christmas at Waltons store in High Street. The local children lined the streets to see Santa ride past on his sleigh and then flocked to visit him at the end of a narrow, but spectacular, grotto. Waltons was demolished in the seventies as part of a relocation of Marks and Spencer to yet another purpose-built store on the corner of Queen Street. The opposite corner was occupied by C&A in premises which caused considerable debate when built in 1970, as it was thought the design was not compatible with the exising architecture.

Shortly before Christmas Exonians gathered in the evenings for community carols sung outside the cathedral where a colourfully lit tree always stood. Another familiar seasonal sight, which everyone visited, was the nativity crib in the window of F.W. Woolworth and also in the bomb-damaged spire of Southernhay Congregational church.

Home refrigerators were still rare in the post-war years so most people did not purchase their turkey or goose for the Christmas dinner until the last minute. The birds were displayed in the shop windows of the local poulterers' and butchers' shops rather than in the deep freeze cabinets of supermarkets.

Leafy High Street. This stretch of road has since been widened to allow more room for buses. Subsequently the trees and flower beds have been removed.

The circus was still a popular attraction during the fifties. Chipperfields, Bertram Mills' and Billy Smart's circuses were regular visitors and the Big Top was usually pitched at Wonford fields. The shows normally travelled by train and traditionally the elephants paraded through the streets from the station to the circus field.

Less animate animals have been a popular attraction at the Albert Memorial Museum in Queen Street for around 100 years. The museum acquired its large collection of stuffed mammals in the early part of the twentieth century. It includes a magnificent Bengal tiger shot by King George V, but the children's favourite remains to this day a giraffe so tall that it stands in a galleried room.

Commercial television was first seen in the city in the late fifties by those connected to the rediffusion cable wireless system but everyone else had to wait for the arrival of Westward TV in 1961. A promotional train, drawn by the now veteran record-breaking locomotive *City of Truro,* visited Exeter in the spring of that year and the station went live in the summer. Local radio took much longer. DevonAir first broadcast from its studios in St David's Hill on 7 November 1980. BBC Radio Devon followed three years later.

For many years Exeter staged two carnivals, in St Thomas and Heavitree. These eventually amalgamated into the hugely popular Exeter carnival procession held annually in October. Sadly this too disappeared in the nineties due to the high financial cost of staging such a spectacular event and the increasing cost of insurance cover for the floats.

As old traditions disappeared others sprang up to replace them. In 1975 the first Exeter Festival was held. This began with a carnival-style parade through the city centre organised by local business organisations. The early festivals were community-based events but gradually it has become much more cultural, featuring concerts by major orchestras. 1982 saw the staging of the first Exeter

The Royal Albert Memorial Museum opened in 1869.

Cowick Street in the early 1960s.

marathon which was won by local athlete Gordon Seward. The attraction of running 26 miles 385 yards waned after a few years and the annual race became a half marathon and is now well established as the Great West Run.

On the political front Exeter returned a Conservative MP until the mid-sixties when Gwyneth Dunwoody won the seat for Labour. Sir John Hannam reclaimed it for the Tories in 1970, retaining it until his retirement in 1997. Former BBC reporter Ben Bradshaw then won the seat for Labour and has become a popular and influential figure in the city.

The construction of the new inner bypass put Exeter onto the front pages of the national newspapers in 1961. The route of Western Way would take the road from the Exe Bridge North via Exe Isle and under New Bridge Street. This plan called for the demolition of Frog Street and with it a medieval house which stood on the junction with Edmund Street Although in a dreadful state of neglect a preservation order was placed on the old house. The only solution was to move it physically to another site. The house was shored up, jacked up on to wheels and winched slowly from the site it had occupied for almost 600 years to a new position opposite St Mary Steps church. The 'house that moved' attracted enormous media interest and has since become a much photographed tourist attraction.

The Quay achieved nationwide television coverage in the early seventies when the BBC drama series *The Onedin Line* was filmed there. This was the story of a Victorian shipping line set in Liverpool with the Exe doubling for the Mersey waterfront.

1974 saw the Royal Devon and Exeter Hospital move to a new site on Barrack Road where the wards were housed in a tower block. The old Georgian building was renamed Dean Clarke House and became the offices of the Exeter Health

Old House in Frog Street, Exeter.

Left: The 'house that moved' before it moved.

Below: The house it replaced.

The 'house that moved' after the move.

Authority. Later the West of England Eye Infirmary also moved to Barrack Road and its former premises were converted into the Hotel Barcelona. Alas the new hospital could not match the longevity of the original and in the nineties it was discovered to have concrete cancer. The tower block was demolished and replaced with a new low-level building.

Throughout the fifties and sixties the Exeter bypass had become notorious nationally for long traffic hold-ups during the summer months. The problem was finally relieved by the arrival of the M5 Birmingham to Exeter motorway in 1976. Twelve months later the M5 was extended across the river and Exminster marshes via a sweeping viaduct. A motorway service area was built at Sowton around which a second major trading estate has grown. Many city businesses have moved out of town to new premises including the *Express and Echo* newspaper which opened state of the art offices and printing facilities while the jewel in the crown was the arrival of the Meteorological Office which was transferred from Bracknell and was officially opened in 2004 to mark 150 years of the 'Met Office'.

Marsh Barton had also spread and is now home to the majority of the city's major car showrooms and workshops. The cattle market made yet another move in the 1980s, this time to the Matford end of Marsh Barton where it became the Exeter Livestock Centre.

The Queen, accompanied by the Duke of Edinburgh, visited the city again in August 1977 as part of her Silver Jubilee celebrations. They returned at Easter 1983 to distribute the Royal Maundy Money at the cathedral. Subsequent visits saw them tour the Devon County Show on its new site at Westpoint, and in 2002 attend a performance by young people in the cathedral on the first day of the Golden Jubilee tour.

Since 1956 the Devon County Show had been held annually at Whipton showground but the need for more space saw it move to the purpose-built

Westpoint complex at Clyst St Mary in 1990. The Whipton site later became the Exeter Arena which opened in 1993, boasting a sports complex which included an athletics stadium, football and rugby pitches and an indoor bowls centre.

In sport Exeter City Football Club have always enjoyed loyal support, despite languishing in the lower reaches of the Football League. Continual years of financial crises took their toll and in 2003 the Grecians were relegated to the Nationwide Football Conference. Happily, the club was taken over by its supporters and the future is looking much brighter, especially when in January 2005, the Grecians were able to wipe out their debts thanks to a third round FA Cup match and replay against Manchester United.

Rugby at the County Ground has always been well supported. In 1963 a representative match against the New Zealand All Blacks attracted a crowd of 23,000. In the nineties rugby went professional and Exeter became the Chiefs, enjoying considerable success on the pitch. 2006 should see Exeter Rugby move to a new ground at Sandygate, the crowd capacity of which will allow the Chiefs to seek promotion to the very highest level.

Exeter's most successful professional sports side is the Falcons, now one of Britain's oldest speedway teams, whose home has also been the County Ground. Since 1947 the Falcons have won four League Championships and numerous other titles. Over the years the Falcons have tracked a host of international stars, including New Zealander Ivan Mauger, probably the greatest rider the sport has

Speedway at the County Ground, 1948.

ever seen. Mauger won the fifth of his six world championships as a Falcon in 1977. Mark Loram is another Exeter asset who won the world championship crown in 2000.

The city's social scene has changed in many ways since the Second World War. Dances at the Civic Hall in Queen Street were replaced by discothèques and nightclubs which started to open in the sixties and seventies.

The popularity of foreign travel saw a considerable increase in traffic at Exeter airport. Concorde became an annual summer visitor, flying supersonic pleasure trips across the Bay of Biscay. Sadly Concorde is no longer flying but the airport continues to act as the temporary base of the crack Red Arrows aerobatic team when they appear at various seaside resorts and air shows in the West Country. In 2004 the airport received its largest ever visitor when a Boeing 747 jumbo jet arrived for a service.

The millennium was marked by a service in the cathedral and the letting off of thousands of fireworks all over the city. A more permanent commemoration was the building of a new footbridge, known as Miller's Crossing, over the Exe at Head Weir.

The last fifty years has seen Exeter undergo more changes and growth than at any other time in its history – the population has grown from 37,718 in 1901 to 111,076 in 2001 – but it has still managed to retain much of its character and remains a pleasant, vibrant place in which to live. The enormous increase in traffic, which occasionally brings Exeter to the verge of gridlock, and the spread of new housing over the surrounding hillsides has not prevented the city from remaining one of the country's most desirable places to live and work – a fact confirmed by spiralling house prices.

At the time of writing Princesshay is about to be demolished and redeveloped. To many Exonians this is a desecration of the city centre, to others a necessary modernisation. During the last 2,000 years many things have altered in Exeter. Numerous buildings have been replaced or destroyed; some have been missed, others have not. The Roman Bath House made way for the Basilica and Forum; in Georgian times the city gates were demolished, apparently without a word of complaint, to make way for traffic. The Princesshay redevelopment is another step along the way.

This may appear to be a negative way in which to end this book. This is not the case, as the Princesshay situation only serves to underline the fact the Exeter has changed constantly and will continue to change throughout its history, and indicates that the people care a great deal about their city and wish to ensure that when change comes it is achieved by the best possible means.

Walk 1

The walk begins outside the Royal Clarence Hotel in the Cathedral Close (facing the hotel).

The Royal Clarence was the first hotel in England (1770) and the restaurant on the right was originally the Exeter Bank. Turning to look towards the cathedral the statue on the green is of Richard Hooker, born in Heavitree around 1553, and was erected in 1907. To your left is St Martin's church, next to which is Mol's Coffee House where Sir Francis Drake, Sir Walter Raleigh and other Devon sea-dogs regularly used to meet.

Walk down past Mol's and continue along the cobbled Close towards Southernhay.

The houses on the left are the homes of the cathedral clergy, with the exception of the Devon and Exeter Institute. Note the wooden door leading into the courtyard between Nos 10 and 11. The end house was badly damaged during the Blitz but has been fully restored. At the end of the row of houses a section of the original earth ramparts is visible through a gateway in the wall.

Passing under the footbridge you come out into Southernhay. Turn right along Southernhay West.

Here many medieval executions took place and you can admire Nosworthy's Regency terraced houses built between 1798 and 1820. The flower and shrub-beds on the central gardens are striking at most times of the year. At the bottom of the slope on the opposite side of the road stands Dean Clarke House, formally the Royal Devon and Exeter Hospital, which first opened in 1742. It is still used as offices for various departments of the Health Authority.

Turn right onto the footpath around the car park, which takes you along the back of the Southgate Hotel.

The hotel car park was originally Holy Trinity yard and was last used to bury victims of the cholera epidemic. The footpath takes you alongside the city wall, where examples of the square cut Roman stonework came be seen. The path

The city wall at South Gate, the former Holy Trinity church is on the left.

leads to South Street and the site of the South Gate. The gate was removed in 1819, but the position of the notorious prison tower can be seen outlined on the pavement in bricks. The former Holy Trinity church on your right is now the White Ensign club. On the opposite side of South Street is the White Hart Hotel, the last of Exeter's great coaching inns.

After crossing South Street climb the stairs to the Yaroslavl Bridge (wheelchair users should cross Western Way via the traffic light controlled crossing and follow signs to the Quay). Follow the walkway which takes you along the city wall then down through the car park; take the path to Quay Hill and thence onto the Quay.

From the bridge the visitor can obtain a view across the old West Quarter. The path leads from the car park down through the site of the Water Gate.

On your right as you reach the Quay is the Custom House, Exeter's first brick building constructed in 1681. The box tower on the left-hand side was known as the King's Chimney and contains the furnace in which contraband tobacco and other confiscated goods were burned.

Ahead of you is the fish market, now an antiques market, with a fine range of old postcards of Exeter, and café. On your left-hand side is the Quay House Interpretation Centre and further along the riverbank are the Victorian warehouses and a row of arches tunnelled into the cliff face which now house a variety of interesting craft shops. On the cliff overlooking the river is Colleton Crescent built between 1802-14 by the Nosworthy brothers, Matthew and Thomas. The Prospect Inn is on your left, or, if you wish to extend your walk, the Port Royal and the suspension bridge are further downstream. You can also cross the river to the Piazza via the historic Butt's Ferry (which has carried Exonians across the river since at least 1750) and return to the Quay via the much more recent Crickelpit Bridge.

From the Quay follow Commercial Road left from the Custom House to Western Way then use the underpass to reach the original medieval bridge.

The ground you are now standing on was once swampy marshland and was first crossed by Nicholas Gervase's stone bridge, several arches of which can still be seen. This area was known as Exe Island and it was here that Exeter's serge industry was located. The remains of St Edmund's church, demolished in the early 1970s, stand at the side of the bridge arches. Gervase was buried in the crypt.

At the city end of the bridge cross Western Way at the pelican crossing. You are now at the site of the West Gate.

Ahead of you, between St Mary Steps church and two sixteenth-century houses, is Stepcote Hill, the narrow medieval route up into the city from the west. It was here that William of Orange and his army entered Exeter in 1688. On your left is the 'house that moved', which was winched to its present location from Frog Street in 1961 to make way for the construction of Western Way. If it is nearly on the hour, wait and watch the Matthew the Miller clock on St Mary Steps church.

Walk up West Street, cross New Bridge Street and continue up Bartholomew Street. Where the road bears right by the Picture House, continue straight up the path along the city wall.

The corner where the wall turns sharply was called the Snayle Tower. This part of Exeter was known as Britayne as it was here that the Britons lived before they were expelled by Althelstan in 928. It was also in this vicinity that Gytha, mother of King Harold, is thought to have lived at the time of the Norman Conquest. From the Snayle Tower visitors can obtain a good view of the River Exe and St Thomas.

Continue along the city wall until you reach Bartholomew Yard.

This became the city's main graveyard in 1637 when it was decided that the cathedral yard was full. It continued to be used until the cholera epidemic of 1832. One of the few remaining memorials is that of John Gidley and his family. Gidley was Exeter's first town clerk and held the office from 1835 until his death in 1865. Below the city wall are the Victorian catacombs, a failed commercial enterprise. Although there was room for thousands of Exonians to be entombed here only a few took advantage of the new facility and the scheme rapidly went bankrupt.

Continue along the pavement to the junction with North Street.

Here the road leads onto the Iron Bridge. Opposite the City Gate Inn can be seen a memorial tablet marking the site of the North Gate, scene of attacks by

Above left: John Gidley's memorial in Bartholomew Yard.

Above right: Stone commemorating the West Gate, sadly showing traces of graffiti.

Perkin Warbeck in 1497 and the Cornish Prayer Book rebels in 1549. Above it, mounted on a grey pole, is a restored weathervane thought to have been mounted on the North Gate and damaged by musket balls during the Civil War. The indentations can still be seen in the right light. It has been suggested that the pole on which the weathervane is mounted is the last remaining tram pole, used to hold the overhead power wires for the electric tram system. Another well-preserved section of the city wall can be viewed in the beer garden of the City Gate pub. A short diversion down the stone steps gives an excellent view of the Iron Bridge, constructed in 1834 to ease the climb for coaches and pack-horses entering the city from the north.

You can experience the climb by retracing your steps and continuing up to the top of North Street.

Until North Street was widened in 1821 this major route into the city from north Devon was just 10ft wide. Exeter's first super cinema – the Gaumont – which opened in 1932, and can be seen through a narrow entrance on the right, is now a popular bingo hall.

On reaching the traffic lights at the top of North Street, turn left into High Street.

This crossroad was the central junction where the major roads met and was the site of the medieval Carfoix, the distribution point for drinking water. It was

119

The junction of North Street, South Street and High Street – this was the site of the Carfoix, the city's main source of drinking water.

here that Sir Thomas St Leger and Thomas Rame were beheaded on the orders of Richard III.

Turn left and walk along High Street, looking out for Parliament Street on the left before you reach the Guildhall.

Parliament Street is said to be the narrowest street in the world, and certainly the narrowest in Exeter. It was a medieval lane from High Street to the now demolished Waterbeer Street and was given its present name in 1832 during the debate surrounding the Reform Act.

The Guildhall is the oldest municipal building in England and is normally open to visitors. Next door to the Guildhall is the Turks Head Inn, a favourite watering hole of Charles Dickens.

Return a short distance down High Street and opposite the entrance to the Guildhall shopping centre turn left into Broadgate which will lead you back to Cathedral Close.

Broadgate was the main gate of the nine which secured the Cathedral Close. It was built on the orders of Edward I following the murder of Precentor Walter

Parliament Street, said
to be the narrowest
street in the world.

Lechlade in 1283. Look out for small brass fittings set in the old kerb stones
along High Street and Broadgate. Into these were fitted the poles which held up
shop sun blinds during the early twentieth century. It was from the Close that
Bram Stoker sent the lawyer Jonathan Harker off to Transylvania in his novel
Dracula.

You can now continue your walk back through the cathedral yard to the
starting point, or take advantage of the many restaurants and cafés in this
area. The cathedral has not been included in these tours as it is assumed that
the visitor will investigate this independently.

Walk 2

Start from the Royal Clarence Hotel. Facing the cathedral turn left into
St Martin's Lane and head towards High Street.

On your right is the Ship Inn, believed to have been a favourite haunt of Sir Francis Drake.

At the junction with High Street cross over (keep a wary eye open for buses
which are still allowed through) and continue ahead down Queen Street.

This junction was the first in Exeter to be controlled by traffic lights, which were installed in 1929. Queen Street was originally called Upper Market Street but renamed at the time of Victoria's coronation. The statue of the Queen Victoria, which originally stood over the market entrance, can now be seen above the much newer Marks and Spencer building. The original market frontage, designed by Charles Fowler and built by the Hoopers in 1838 has now been incorporated in the Guildhall shopping centre. A few hundred yards further along on the right-hand side is the Albert Memorial Museum. At the rear of which, in Gandy Street, is the Phoenix Arts Centre. This building originally housed the University of the South West.

Continue past the museum to the end of the block and turn right into
Northernhay Gardens.

Opposite the Northernhay entrance gate is the former Exeter Dispensary. To the right of this is the Thistle Hotel (formerly Rougemont Hotel) which stands on the site occupied in the early nineteenth century by the city gaol. Alongside and below the gardens is Central station, known as Queen Street station when it was built in 1868. The City War Memorial, designed by John Angel, stands a short distance from the gate. The city wall runs on your right and there can be seen the statue of Sir Thomas Acland, who travelled on the first train from Exeter St David's to London in 1844.

At the War Memorial turn right, go through the gateway in Athelstan's Tower and
follow the path around the mound of Rougemont Castle to the Norman gateway.

Rougemont House, which stands close by the Norman gatehouse, was built by John Patch, a surgeon at the Devon and Exeter Hospital, in about 1770. Patch was also a keen gardener and created the gardens around the castle.

Northernhay, Queen Street Entrance, Exeter.

Entrance to Northernhay Gardens.

Walk down Castle Street to High Street.

You are now entering an area which was virtually totally destroyed by enemy bombing in May 1942. On your right is the telephone exchange which was one of the few buildings which survived. It was saved from destruction by the bravery of the fire watchers who threw burning incendiary bombs from the roof as the staff at the switchboards battled to keep the lines open. Not so fortunate was the old City Library on the opposite corner. This was burnt out along with thousands of books.

Castle Street.

Turn left into High Street and continue to the site of the East Gate. This can be found opposite Boots the Chemist. Cross High Street and follow the course of the city wall which is marked by a line of bricks in the pavement.

A brass plaque marks the site of the East Gate and close by is the booking kiosk which provides details of the current shows at the Northcott Theatre. If you wish to explore Exeter's medieval passages, the entrance is in Roman Gate Passage adjacent to Boots. Just beyond the ticket kiosk is the Phoenix Fountain, erected in memory of the Blitz.

Continue past the corner tower of the city wall and turn right into Southernhay.

From here can be seen the spire which was the only part of Southernhay Congregational (now United Reform) church which survived the Blitz. Chichester Place, another example of Exeter's Regency building boom, built by William Hooper in 1824-5 was also fortunate to survive intact.

Continue past Broadwalk House, built in the early seventies, and turn right into Bedford Street.

On the left-hand side is Fanum House, formerly the Automobile Association offices, which stand on the site of the first Bedford Theatre which burnt down in 1820. Bedford Street was originally the site of the Black Friars (Dominican) house. In 1539 the dissolution of the monasteries saw the friary become

Bedford House, the home of Lord John Russell, Duke of Bedford. It was here that Princess Henrietta, the daughter of Charles I, was born on 1 May 1644.

Continue back to High Street. At this junction stood the famous Deller's Café, which was destroyed in 1942. Turn left, then after 100 yards turn left again under St Stephen's Bow.

On your right is the rear entrance of Dingles, formerly the fashionable Colsons store founded by Mrs Colson, a war widow, in 1789.

Turn right along Catherine Street back into Cathedral Close.

It is hoped that you enjoyed these walks. If you would like to further explore Exeter we recommend the Redcoat Guides. These guided walks, which are free, mainly start from outside the Royal Clarence and details are displayed nearby.

Index